I0070003

Do DEI Right

Do DEI Right

*Cut Through the Noise and
Drive Lasting Results*

by
Michelle Bogan Feferman

PYP **Publish** Your Purpose

Publish Your Purpose
141 Weston Street, #155
Hartford, CT, 06141

Publish
Your Purpose

The opinions expressed by the Author are not necessarily those held by Publish Your Purpose.

Ordering Information: Quantity sales and special discounts are available on quantity purchases by corporations, associations, and others. For details, contact the author at hello@equity-at-work.com.

Edited by: August Li, Anna Heim
Cover design by: Rebecca Pollock
Typeset by: Amit Dey
Author Photo by Tamytha Cameron

ISBN: 979-8-88797-171-1 (hardcover)
ISBN: 979-8-88797-173-5 (paperback)
ISBN: 979-8-88797-174-2 (ebook)
Library of Congress Control Number: 2025909195

First edition, October 2025.

Publish Your Purpose is a hybrid publisher of non-fiction books. Our mission is to elevate the voices often excluded from traditional publishing. We intentionally seek out authors and storytellers with diverse backgrounds, life experiences, and unique perspectives to publish books that will make an impact in the world. Do you have a book idea you would like us to consider publishing? Please visit PublishYourPurpose. com for more information.

"Make a career of humanity. Commit yourself to the noble struggle for equal rights. You will make a better person of yourself, a greater nation of your country, and a finer world to live in."

—Dr. Martin Luther King Jr.

My vision for every workplace:

The benefits of a diverse workforce are recognized and embraced in all industries and in all sizes of organizations.

Differences are celebrated, valued, and acknowledged for creating rich work cultures, fostering meaningful relationships, and driving innovation, growth, and financial success.

Every process in an employee's lifecycle is equitable and focused on unlocking each person's full potential.

Inclusion is the norm.

This book is dedicated to every person working to make this vision a reality.

TABLE OF CONTENTS

HOW I CAME TO THIS WORK

There is a story my grandmother loved to tell about me. When I was three years old, she and my grandfather took my parents, aunt, uncle, and me on a family trip. I was the only kid. One day we were packing up for a picnic, and I declared that I wanted to spread the peanut butter on the sandwiches "all by myself." When we went somewhere in the car, I would declare again that I wanted to buckle the seatbelt "all by myself." I wanted to prove I could do it and that I didn't need help. Independence was a quality I was born with.

That drive for independence and the qualities I developed to make it happen (resourcefulness, being strategic and a big-picture thinker, empathy, relationship builder, and creativity) are the things that propelled me forward in all aspects of my life. I was determined to find *my* path, not just pick a standard one. From as early an age as twelve, I started working. Getting a small taste of financial freedom was like adding jet fuel to the plan. I found the means to my independence.

And I worked my tail off from that moment on. I always held multiple jobs while going to school and applied for every honors scholarship I could. I saved like mad, and once I graduated from UC Berkeley, I accepted an offer to model in Europe as my ticket to see more of the world. I expected to be there six weeks at most and wanted this experience before committing myself to a corporate career. And while I never made great money, I ended up making enough to keep going for over two years after undergrad, moving all over Europe and South Africa. I went over, not knowing a soul, and figured it out. I landed jobs, found places to live, traveled for work and fun, made friends, dated, and learned new languages, cultures, foods, and currencies. Taking myself out of everything familiar was a way for me to strip down to my core, learn from how people lived in other parts of the world, define the tenets that were important for me to live by, and be intentional about how I would show up in the world. Questioning assumptions, applying critical thinking, and speaking the truth were at the top of my list and have had a big influence on me personally and professionally ever since.

This was in the mid-1990s, the age of "heroin chic" in the modeling scene, and there was constant pressure to do drugs, perform sexual favors for work, starve oneself, or be bulimic to succeed. Meanwhile, I preferred clean living, such as going to museums and parks, reading, and eating. Once, I was fired from a job because I wouldn't sleep with the photographer. Saying no to him made me feel strong, even though it cost me any further work through that agency. The head of the agency sat me down and told me that my decision not to sleep with that photographer proved I wasn't willing to do what it takes to be successful as a model. Luckily, I wasn't banking on modeling for my career.

As time went on and what I wanted for my life became clearer, I grew tired of a job that valued being quiet and looking pretty to sell other people's things. I became eager to make a mark in the business world and grow my skills there. I moved back to Los Angeles, where I grew up, and started my job search. Transitioning from modeling to a corporate job was not easy. Even as a UC Berkeley graduate, I often got interviewed just to see what I looked like (this was before people had digital photos online). After eight months of temping at multiple companies, I finally landed an entry-level corporate job and felt I was on my way. I was determined to learn and prove my worth quickly, believing hard work, dedication, and smarts would create opportunities for me. In the eighteen months I spent there, I learned that, at least at that organization, how hard I worked was not relevant. My dedication did not matter. Smarts were only meaningful if they got you a graduate degree from a short list of schools; without that, there would be no consideration for advancement. The final straw for me was discovering multiple people were having affairs with other people at work as a way to get ahead and that this was a known and accepted practice. It felt like I was back in the modeling world all over again.

While I found this upsetting and disheartening, I was sure that if I found the "right" place to work, sticking to my values would lead to success. I was hungry for more experience, so I zeroed in on what I wanted to do next and networked like crazy to get interviews and make it happen. I landed a job in retail consulting and moved to New York City. My boyfriend was from New York and was thrilled to move back there with me, and we moved in together. It was a new city, a new job, all new people, and a ton to learn. I loved it. I felt like my brain was operating at full speed all the time, and it was a rush. I was working with senior people in the industry and learning how they thought. It was brilliant.

I worked in a very collegial environment that was friendly and open, so it felt very supportive. There was an intensity to the relationships there because we worked long hours together and traveled extensively. The collegiality created a fun atmosphere that spilled over into social time often. At first this felt really foreign to me, as I had kept my work and personal lives separate until then. But over time it became more natural, and work friends became personal friends. I started to see the power of relationships.

A year and a half later, my boyfriend and I got engaged and married in 2000. Once I got married, I started to notice that some of the older male partners treated me differently. It was as if a few of them had gotten together and placed a bet on how long before I left to start a family, as if I couldn't do my job and have a child at the same time. A few openly talked about it, but it was always spun as a joke. Between that and how much more senior the men were, along with the degree of control they had over my future at the firm, I never said anything. Our former CEO once joked to a client in front of me that he made me promise I wouldn't get pregnant during a project. I was so happy when we didn't get that work.

Once I advanced into a manager role, I began to see bad behavior around the firm, particularly in how the women were treated compared to the men. There were whispers about strip club outings after training sessions for the men, as well as frequent male-only invites for nights out drinking. The women worked hard and started to band together, but it was such a patriarchal environment, and the old boys' club was so strong, it was hard to create any change. The more senior women, even the outstanding performers, were always the first to go when layoffs or staff reshuffling occurred. Some of the up-and-coming, top-performing women left preemptively once they saw this pattern emerging.

Seven years into my time at the firm, I was working tirelessly to prove I was ready for promotion to partner. For that to happen, I needed three years of consistently high performance in specific sales and delivery metrics. I had strong performance and a reputation as a go-to person who could deliver excellent results for clients and drive internal projects forward. What I did not have was a steady three-year streak, because I had taken maternity leave for my first child, Grace. And those criteria were set in stone. I was passed over that year and told I needed at least another eighteen months of consistently high marks to even be considered, since I had taken "a break." I'd love to meet a new parent who considers their parental leave a break. Talk about being detached from reality. Coming back to work was my break.

I had tried to prepare myself for this, but it still burned. Unfortunately, there were so few female partners (we never had more than 13 percent of our partner level represented by women) that no one was in a position to advocate on my behalf. The general understanding among staff was that our firm was not serious about getting women to the partner level and keeping them there. So I fought. And fought. I had to nearly disregard my family for the eighteen months following my maternity leave, traveling nonstop and even taking my one-year-old with me to be babysat in other cities when we didn't have care at home. But I was determined, and I finally made it. I was promoted to be the youngest partner at the firm at the time, one of a handful of women at that level globally.

In the meantime, in one-on-one client meetings, I encountered more inappropriate behavior from male clients. My colleagues were reticent to say anything in my support because of our "the client is always right" mantra. They felt bad for me, but stepping in to reinforce that what the client did was inappropriate or out of line never happened. I did not feel like I could push back as directly as I wanted to with clients who crossed the line, or got too close to the line, until I knew my new partner position at the firm was secure. Which, given how few women we had, did not have a likelihood of happening any time soon.

Then came the hit I never could have seen coming.

July 2, 2009, was the day my life changed. Completely, fully, in every way imaginable. The entire foundation my life was built upon vanished when I came home one afternoon.

I was living in a suburb of Boston at the time and had gone into the city to get my hair cut. It was a Thursday. I was home on maternity leave with my son Jack, and my husband was going to keep Grace, who had just turned three, and Jack, who was three months old, while I went into the city. I had organized a daddy playdate for him and a good friend's father, who was also home with his kids, who were close in age, at that friend's house. Another dad was also going to stop by with his two kids.

On my way home from my haircut, my husband called and said he was on his way home from the playdate. I would be home within twenty minutes of him getting home, maximum.

Usually, I would run errands on my way home from Boston, but something in my gut told me not to do that, to just head home. I got home and came into the house through our basement entrance, the main entrance we used every day to come in from the driveway and garage. I shut the door and heard a yelp come from Jack, a noise I had never heard before and one that shot straight up my spine. My legs started to move automatically, and I ran up the stairs to the main floor, around into the sunroom, where I heard my husband screaming at Jack and saw him leaning on Jack with all his body weight, Jack propped up in the corner of the couch. My husband's full body weight was on Jack, with him pushing one hand on Jack's tiny chest and the other hand smothering his mouth. He was screaming in Jack's face.

I started yelling at my husband, "Stop it! Get off! You're hurting him!" He didn't react at all, didn't appear to see or hear me. I tried to pull him off Jack and could not move him. It was like he was possessed with a rage that gave him superhuman strength. I tried again and was able to get him off this time. I got Jack out from under him and ran away into another room. I checked Jack, and he seemed miraculously okay. I tried to get him to settle. Jack was beet red, screaming and crying. Then my husband came up and told me, in a completely calm manner, that he was going to the gym, and he left.

I was in total shock.

What just happened?

Did I imagine that?

Is Jack okay? Where is Grace? Is she okay?

About ninety minutes later, my husband came home and was completely shocked that I was upset. I told him that if he didn't think what he did was wrong, he could not live with us. Showing absolutely no emotion—no anger, no remorse, no sadness—he went upstairs, packed a duffel bag, and left.

I felt like someone pulled the rug out from under me, and I was sent free-falling into a black hole, scrambling to hold my sweet babies and grab onto anything that would safely steady us. Everything in my personal life changed in that instant.

At this point, I was one month away from the end of my maternity leave. As the reality of my new situation sank in, I looked to work for some stability. Having been at my firm for ten years and consistently receiving feedback that I was highly valued and a top performer, in addition to having many great personal relationships with the leadership team, I thought surely they would give me some flexibility when I had to return. After all, I now had to manage this new life (all that was now required for safety, legal, mental, and physical health, and more) on my own, with no family close by and with no local office within a four-hour drive.

"Could I come back but not travel right away," I asked our CEO, "even for just six weeks while I try to steady things?"

"No."

A hard no, not delivered by phone or in person, but in a terse email by one of the senior leaders who was always touting our firm's supportive, family-like culture. I was a partner. The firm needed me to come back and get on the road right away to sell and oversee the delivery of work. It was 2009, and the economy was in bad shape. The firm was concerned about performance. And that was all I got.

I had given so much to the firm: working endless long days, nights, and weekends; nonstop travel; taking on internal leadership roles on top of meeting my sales and delivery goals; and coaching and mentoring so many people. Couldn't the firm give me a little grace in return?

"No."

I was devastated.

Here I was, getting the locks on my house changed and having friends' husbands look after us, starting a job search. With no job leads nearby, it quickly became clear I would have to move for a new position. This also meant I couldn't file for divorce yet, because my husband could have petitioned the court to keep me from moving, and then I'd be unemployed while caring for my kids. I had no legal protection while we were in this limbo state because I couldn't file for divorce in a new state until I was a legal resident there, which would take six months to a year, depending on the state.

Fortunately, as I started to get the word out that I was looking for a new job, a client of mine reached out with a compelling offer. They wanted to hire me and would pay to relocate us to New York. My legal battles were only beginning, but at least this would give me a well-paying job and a home for myself and my children. I could exhale, just a tiny bit.

While it was far from easy, I worked hard to be everything for my children and continue to have a career. I needed that, and so did they. I had an amazing boss at the new job who is still a dear friend to this day. He supported, pushed, and advocated for me, creating a safe harbor at a time when I desperately needed it. I had a good team, and we accomplished meaningful things for the company.

The missing piece, however, was a good culture. It was a kill-or-be-killed corporate environment, where people commonly threw each other under the bus and sabotaged others' success. Yelling and backstabbing were commonplace. There was very little trust. People could be lovely personally and then turn on you in a meeting. These issues were not about bias or misogyny, but equal-opportunity bad behavior was no more tolerable. I had to be on my guard constantly. One day, I realized I was talking to myself as I walked toward the employee entrance, telling myself I could get through another day. I was a forty-year-old executive, for crying out loud. I realized it was time to go.

Changing jobs but staying in New York City would most likely result in the same problems with a different name on the door. I needed a break from another toxic work environment, from my now ex-husband, who was unstable and dangerous, from the grind of commuting into New York City, and from the brutal cost of raising two children as a single parent there. A dear friend from childhood came into town for my birthday, and my brother flew in as a surprise. They both lived in Dallas. That was my sign. We could move to Dallas! I flew down, bought a house, came back to New York, quit my job, and then took a breath. My gut told me those were the imperative steps. Now what would I do for work?

In an unlikely turn of events, my old firm asked me to come back, saying they had done a lot to change the culture, get more women into senior roles, and treat people better. I still had many friends there, and they confirmed that changes were significant and working. Several of the key "bad seeds" retired (or were asked to retire), and that opened the door for some more serious change to happen. They offered me a great role and the flexibility to work remotely, traveling as needed, but on a schedule I dictated. At this point I knew I had nothing to lose. I was moving to Texas with or without a job and knew I could get another job if this one did not pan out. I was exhausted from my divorce and caring for my children under such challenging circumstances. Friends at work would be a salve. I decided to take it.

Things were better, and as a senior partner I certainly had more input and leverage at the firm overall. At the same time, because of my seniority, the instances of bias were much clearer because now I could see them play out across teams, offices, and practice areas. Bias and mistreatment were happening to employees who were female, LGBTQIA+, and people of color. Not as directly as before, but it was definitely still there.

The difference then, in 2014, was awareness of bias in the workplace was rising. Employees were organizing and speaking up. We formed our first internal network for women and started to tackle this head-on, ultimately becoming an avenue of advocacy for anyone who was not of the old boys' club mold. It took persistent, intentional work over several years, but the tide started to change, and we created policies and processes that ensured people of all kinds of backgrounds and life experiences could succeed, even when they needed flexibility for personal reasons. A place where I could have stayed after the tragedy that befell my family five years earlier.

My children and I would ultimately have to move three more times and endure countless legal, mental health, and financial challenges before we could be fully safe from my ex-husband. If my firm had just given me a little time, it would have saved my children and me so much heartache, stress, upheaval, and financial devastation. All I asked for was six weeks to work from home. So miniscule in the grand scheme of things.

Looking back on this, I realized later that I believed moving into a corporate role would provide a structure with rules and ways of working that would provide safety and security. I assumed corporate work would lay out a clear path to success where hard work, intelligence, integrity, and savvy would reap honest rewards. It took a while for me to understand that it can, but it is not a given by any means.

I was also perplexed and frustrated that there were all these systems in place to standardize progress. It seemed counterintuitive to me and didn't always align well with rewarding hard work, dedication, and delivering great results, especially the further into my career I got. At first I thought it was something I was doing wrong, that if I just worked harder or got the right champions on my side, it would change things. I was progressing, but not as fast as male peers who were not as accomplished as me. In the years of being engaged, married, and then pregnant, it became crystal clear I was being treated differently because I was a woman, and that it was a systemic issue, not something specific to me.

Gaining clarity on that made everything click into place for me. I could not accept the limitations systemic bias creates, for myself or for anyone else. I saw too many talented people get burned by this, resulting in them quitting, stalling out, becoming depressed, or behaving in a toxic manner as a defense mechanism. They suffered, and the organizations they worked for suffered.

I am on a mission to break the cycle of bias, and that is the essence of diversity, equity, and inclusion (DEI) work. No one can be seen, heard, and valued within a system that is assumed to be fair but is actually stacked against them. As I scanned the market for solutions, I did not find the kind of help I knew organizations needed to address these issues and achieve sustainable change. That is what led me to step off the corporate track and found Equity At Work™, helping organizations create environments where every employee can have a voice and have the opportunity to reach their full desired potential.

This book captures all I have learned over the past twenty years of doing this work as part of leadership roles inside companies and as a DEI consultant to other organizations. I have seen what works, what does not work, what makes this hard, what is needed for long-term success, and more. I will share everything so you can benefit from all the lessons learned along the way and craft your own DEI plan that will have a major impact in your organization.

The book is organized around the Equity At Work™ DEI Maturity Model I developed that my team and I have used with organizations across industries of all sizes, public and private. I will walk you through setting the foundation for DEI, then operationalizing DEI, and finally, continuously improving your DEI work. I will show you how to develop a strategy, build a roadmap, and establish accountabilities and metrics. Examples of policies, benefits, processes, programs, and training will be provided throughout the book. Finally, I will share best practices, lessons learned, and stories so you can see how others have successfully embedded DEI into the DNA of their organizations.

There is a compelling business case for DEI work, and that is important to ground your plans in. Where the business case gets real is when great changes happen for individuals: someone getting promoted who would not have before, or being able to come out at work and share their personal life more fully, or getting a job they would not have been considered for previously. These are the most meaningful moments for me, the ones that drive me to keep working every day. Seeing the personal impact and the ripple effect on their families, networks, and communities is a profound experience. My goal in writing this book is to help you make those moments happen in your organization too.

This work gets to the lifeblood of an organization. It is precious, delicate, and essential. It affects every person in the organization. It takes intentional, deliberate focus with a sustained commitment over time. And it is completely doable. When you see the spark of a change that gives someone an opportunity for the first time, you will feel how incredibly rewarding this work can be. I can't imagine a better way to spend my working time than to help drive those changes, help lift up employees, and pass on what I have learned to you.

Let's get to it!

CHAPTER 1

WHAT IS DEI?
HOW DOES IT SHOW UP AT WORK?

On May 25, 2020, George Floyd, a forty-six-year-old Black American man, was murdered in Minneapolis by Derek Chauvin, a forty-four-year-old white police officer. Witnesses who recorded the incident on their phones captured Derek pinning George, who was unarmed, to the ground and placing his knee on George's neck for nine minutes and twenty-nine seconds. George repeatedly said "I can't breathe," "Please," and "Mama" before dying. George's crime? Making a purchase using a $20 bill suspected of being counterfeit.

George's murder set off a national uprising against police violence and systemic racism. This was the largest anti-racism movement since the civil rights protests of the 1960s. In the workplace, it triggered a widespread movement to address bias and inequality. This initially focused on race and then expanded to include many dimensions of diversity. All of a sudden, the general public in the US became familiar with the term "DEI"—short for diversity, equity, and inclusion—as well as the concept of unconscious bias, and many of the disparities faced by historically underrepresented minority employees and job seekers. There was a rush to support Black Lives Matter and other social justice movements. Many business leaders were determined to fix systemic racism quickly. Surely if they devoted time and resources to this work, it could all be fixed and we could return to business, right? Wrong.

Even with the best of intentions, leaders learned that this was not quick, easy work. Many companies hurried to put out statements in support of Black Lives Matter. However, those that did not live out what was in those statements internally with employees were quickly called out for being everything from performative to misleading to two-faced. There was a rush to recruit from Historically Black Colleges and Universities (HBCUs), but often without a long-term commitment to those institutions or first doing the work internally to make sure new employees with different educational backgrounds would be set up for success. There were many requests for unconscious bias training, which is important, but only impactful within the context of broader DEI work, a context that was typically missing.

The lesson here is not that these communications, recruiting, or training steps were wrong; it is that they were done in the hopes that they would provide a quick fix. It takes intention, thoughtfulness, and commitment to create change, and DEI work is no different. It is tough because it focuses on behavior, language, and how we work together every day. This is also why it can be so positively impactful when done right.

There are many well-researched benefits to DEI. I will cover all the ways your work can drive these benefits, for your people and your organization, throughout the book. Some of the benefits I see most often are captured here:

These proven benefits yield a strong ROI for DEI work

Every 1% increase in gender diversity yields a **3% increase in revenue**[1]

The top 25% of racially diverse companies are 33% more likely to **outperform on EBIT margin**[2]

Diverse companies are 1.7x more likely to be **innovation leaders**[3]

Diverse teams are 70% more likely to **capture new markets**[4]

Inclusive workplaces **outperform S&P 500 stock performance** by 4x[5]

Diverse and inclusive workplaces have 5.4x **higher employee retention**[5]

Sources: 1) The Female Quotient 2018; 2) McKinsey & Co. 2020; 3) Reset by Deloitte 2015; 4) Harvard Business Review 2013; 5) Great Place To Work 2019

Where do these benefits come from? Largely from environments that welcome, support, and integrate diverse views on opportunities and risk. That sounds simple, but it takes a lot of intentionality to create. But when done right, you break up—or better yet, prevent—groupthink, and then, innovation can truly blossom. Employees love these environments because they feel their ideas matter, so they are highly engaged, want to stay for a long time, and recruit their friends and family members to come work there.

So, what is the best way to "do DEI?" Let's start by defining what DEI is and how it shows up in the workplace.

WHAT IS DIVERSITY?

Time and again, when I have discussions about DEI, people discussing the "D" component go right to race or gender, often as separate elements. Sexual orientation might be the third piece, but it is usually behind the first two.

Race, gender, and sexual orientation are absolutely important diversity demographics, but they are by no means the only ones. None of us can be described by only one dimension.

Diversity is a measure of differences among a group, and those differences can exist across any number of lines. Someone can be in the minority in one group and the majority in another, based on the demographics of those around them. Within the realm of DEI in the workplace, diversity is typically focused on demographic dimensions. The dimensions that typically come to mind are the protected classes that have been defined in the US by the Equal Employment Opportunity Commission as parts of an employee's identity that cannot be discriminated against:

- Race or characteristics associated with a particular race
- Color, pigmentation, or skin color complexion
- National origin or ancestors' place of origin
- Religion, including religious observances, practices, and beliefs
- Sex, including pregnancy, childbirth, or related medical conditions; sexual orientation; and gender identity

- Age (forty or older)
- Disability (temporary and permanent, visible and invisible)
- Genetic information, including family makeup and family medical history

Unless you are a human resources professional, many of these characteristics likely do not come to mind when you think of diversity. But remember, anything that is part of a person's identity is considered when defining diversity. If you think of how you define yourself and what informs how you show up in the world and at work, many of these characteristics likely come to mind. Some of them, such as race, gender, and age, are demographic data you are required to provide to your employer if your employer has more than fifty employees. Some employers will also provide an option, either at the time of hiring or later, as a census or self-identification campaign, for you to share your sexual orientation, disabilities, and veteran status. In many organizations, employees may not feel comfortable sharing those pieces of information out of fear of being treated differently, even if laws protect them against discrimination. If you are collecting that data, you will need to consider whether this is the case and adjust your data as representative or directional accordingly.

Diversity is not limited to protected classes, however. It expands to experiences, personal views, affiliations, and more, because it includes anything that is part of how you define yourself. A tool I use with clients to help them think beyond race, gender, and other protected classes is a diversity wheel, shown here:

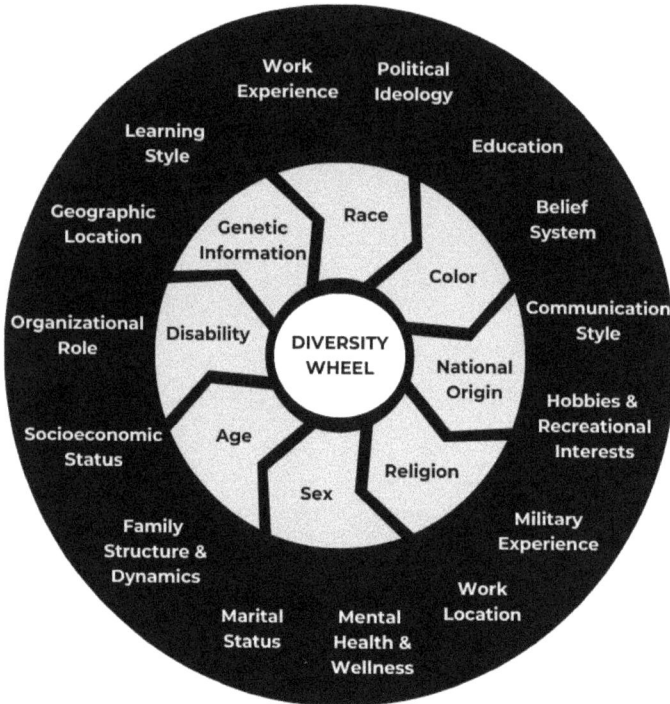

The center circle includes many of the demographics collected by employers. Several of these are also things you may think you know about someone based on how they look, talk, dress, or items they have in their office or virtual background. The outer circle elements are many of the experiences, beliefs, and characteristics that also define who we are. Time and again, when people do not have something in common in the center circle, something they share in the outer circle creates a bridge to connect with others.

This wheel by no means captures all the characteristics that define any one of us, but it does remind us that we are all complex, multidimensional individuals. A term related to DEI that captures this is "intersectionality." Intersectionality was coined in 1989 by Kimberlé Crenshaw as a way to define the compounding effect of multiple parts of a person's identity. Just as each dimension of diversity defines us, it can also be a source of bias from someone who views that dimension negatively. A gay Black man, for example, may experience bias as a gay man and as a Black person, and those compound to have a negative impact greater than that of being gay or being Black.

Keeping this wheel on hand as you plan your DEI initiatives will help you be inclusive of everyone's needs. It will also help you determine where employees who identify with certain dimensions may need greater support than others, especially if they are one of the few, or only, of a particular diversity dimension.

WHAT IS EQUITY? AND WHY FOCUS ON EQUITY INSTEAD OF EQUALITY?

Equity has many meanings, including financial (the equity invested in a house or an equity stake in a business), personal time and work investment (sweat equity), legal (protecting rights to reach equitable settlements), and fairness (just and equitable treatment of people). Fair and just treatment is the focus of equity in DEI, ensuring everyone is provided the support they need to put them on a level playing field with their peers. In the workplace, it is a recognition that all employees start from different places, and adjustments, accommodations, and training may be needed to set employees up for success.

Thinking back to the diversity wheel, all the things that make us unique can create advantages in some settings and disadvantages in others. For example, an employee who is hard of hearing may struggle to hear everything in a meeting if they are not provided preferential seating and/or someone providing sign language. That same employee, because they are hard of hearing, may be exceptional at reading body language and the mood or energy in a room. Providing support to them eliminates the disadvantage in that situation and enables them to contribute in the same way as peers who are not hard of hearing. It also enables them to share their gift of reading the room with those around them.

The reason we do not use equality here is that equality means we treat everyone, regardless of their differences, in the same manner. If someone starts from a place of disadvantage and is treated equally to a person with an advantage, the gap between them is perpetuated and will ultimately grow over time as the advantaged person gains access to more opportunities. However, when equitable measures are put in place to close those gaps, everyone can contribute equally.

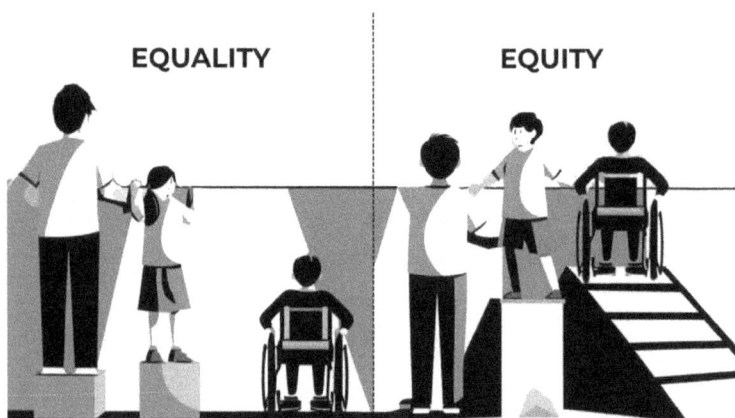

EQUALITY   **EQUITY**

Equality is the end goal of equity. We want to demonstrate that we value everyone's differences and provide the support needed so everyone can perform to their fullest potential. It is a commitment to not let bias interfere with any employee's ability to contribute. It ensures everyone has an opportunity to have a voice, a vote, and a seat at the table. Focusing on equity is a win for employees and for companies, because when everyone is performing at their top level, they are making their best possible contribution to their employer.

WHAT IS INCLUSION?

Inclusion in DEI means ensuring everyone feels they belong. It is equity in action, enabling everyone to feel seen, valued, and heard as their full selves. In my work, I conduct listening sessions with my clients' employees. I frequently hear that employees feel they cannot be open about an important part of their identity, whether it be that they identify as part of the LGBTQIA+ community, that they have a health issue, that they are struggling to support a loved one while working, or something else. When employees have to hide parts of themselves, they are drained energetically and are not able to contribute to their full potential. Their engagement drops, and both they and the organization suffer as a result.

Inclusion comes about in big and small ways. The big part is making it part of your organization's mission and core values. Often, though, those are just words on a website or a wall. The small ways are the ones that make a big difference. They show thoughtfulness and a focus on employees as people, not as resources or labor costs, in day-to-day activities and interactions.

Inclusion embraces the "platinum rule." Many of us are familiar with the golden rule of treating others as you would want to be treated. The platinum rule says we should treat others as they want to be treated. Which means we need to get to know them and really listen. Empathy is a critical skill here. Inclusion can only come from taking the perspective of others and seeking to understand what they need in order to feel like they belong just as they are. To do this, employers need to seek out input, actively listen, be open to feedback, and share back what they have heard and what they will put in place to meet the needs that surfaced. You don't need to agree with someone to empathize with them. You just need to be curious, listen, and reflect on what you have heard to make sure you got it right. This is all about building trust.

A tool my team and I developed and use with clients to help them practice inclusion is an Inclusion Bingo card. This has twenty-five ways that all of us, whether leaders or individual contributors, can be inclusive every day, with the platinum rule right in the center.

Scan the QR code to access English and Spanish digital versions of the Inclusion Bingo card:

Password: DoDEIRight

INCLUSION
BINGO

Show curiosity by listening intently, making eye contact and asking questions	Share your story so others with similar experiences can feel safe sharing too	Check your language and avoid phrases that can be discriminatory or harmful	Make an intentional effort to meet people from other teams	Ask for input to understand different points of view and experiences
Make sure your workplace has accommodations in place for multiple visible and invisible disabilities	Spot your unconscious biases by recognizing and correcting your assumptions	Be a vocal, action-oriented champion of DEI so you role model that behavior for others	Shine a light on colleagues who go above and beyond	Take a partnership approach to differences by finding common ground and collaborating
Be open to feedback to understand how the impact of your words can differ from your intentions	Advocate for another employee to be considered for a special project or role	TREAT OTHERS AS THEY WANT TO BE TREATED	Create a code of conduct for offsite events to make sure everyone can feel safe and included	When someone is facing a challenge, ask them how you can best support them
Be humble by opening up about things you can do better and commit to following through	When speaking to a colleague use their chosen pronouns - and if you don't know what they are, ask	Create space and opportunities for people who are introverted, to contribute their ideas	Make sure others feel heard by validating what they say	Ensure diversity is represented in all outreach efforts: recruiting, community service, events
When someone opens up to you, express gratitude and honor any request for privacy	Be kind by being caring and compassionate in your words and actions	Provide confidential ways to make suggestions on how to make work more inclusive	Focus on qualities and skills, not "fit" to make hiring, assignment, and promotion decisions	Don't assume you know if someone wants to take on a new responsibility - let them decide

There are a lot of creative ways to use this card: as a tool to use with an accountability partner to help you focus on trying a couple specific things; as a team activity; as part of a company-wide inclusion challenge; or by creating your own version with actions you want your employees to take in your organization. However you decide to use it, remember that, just as you may bring diversity to one group and not another, employees can feel included in one setting and not in another. Inclusion is situational, so focus on the situations that are most important for your employees to feel included, and expand from there. It takes each of us being intentional for inclusion to be felt consistently across teams, levels, functions, and locations.

Additionally, inclusion sounds like something that should be easy for all of us to do, but it is a very different approach to work than we have had historically. In the old days, there were pretty firm boundaries between work and personal life. Now those lines are significantly blurred. The shift to remote work that came during COVID cast a light on how common it was for employees to be masking something at work and the strain that was causing them. Almost overnight, we had a window into each other's living situations, family dynamics, health issues, pet needs, and more. The days of checking the personal stuff at the door when going to work were over.

That was and continues to be a real challenge for many leaders who grew up professionally in an era where work and personal life each existed in their own silos. They struggle with how to lead inclusively, not only because they did not have role models for this as they came up the ranks, but also because this feels like it flies in the face of productivity.

Taking time to listen to employees sounds time-consuming, and it may seem like it will get in the way of efficiency.

How can we all hit our target goals when we have to stop to make sure everyone is feeling okay? I can tell you from experience that taking the time to listen, creating safe spaces for tough conversations, and gathering input from employees at all levels actually drives productivity. My most successful clients, measured by their revenue, margin, and competitive performance, are highly inclusive, making DEI part of their DNA. Why? That level of commitment to their employees makes those employees loyal and engaged in their work, driving stellar results for the company while reducing the many costs of turnover.

WHAT ELSE IS DEI CALLED? WHY?

Ultimately, for DEI to be successful in your organization, it needs to align with your specific mission, values, and culture. For some companies, this means changing the terms to emphasize a particular area of focus. Some organizations include "Belonging" as part of DEI, calling it DEIB. Others have incorporated Justice, calling it DEIJ, or added Accessibility and named it DEIA. Some have even dropped Diversity and wrapped it into equity and inclusion. The right way here is to determine what your needs and priorities are, and how this can improve or enhance your culture, and name the work accordingly.

For some organizations, DEI has become a charged term, so they call the work something else altogether. I have clients who are in full "stealth mode" and refer to the work as Culture and Engagement, or simply Inclusion, all of which are terms and concepts that are difficult to argue against. If staying away from charged terms helps you get the work done, do it. One word of caution: if your workforce includes a significant number of Gen Z employees, they are likely looking for DEI to be part of their work experience, as most consider it to be table stakes. If you go too stealth, they may miss that you have elements of DEI in your policies and programs. You will need to balance the needs of all employees when you determine the name and the scope of your work.

WHERE TO GO FROM HERE

Before embarking on your DEI strategy, roadmap, or other initiatives, it is important to identify what DEI means to you and your leaders personally. Similar to the diversity wheel exercise, there are elements of DEI that are especially important to each of us. We have to figure out where we each fit in this work and what we bring to the table before leading the charge for others. A great way to do this is through an exercise called "My Story."

I was first introduced to this concept by my colleague Dr. Robert Simmons III[1], a gifted and impactful DEI leader and educator. In his view, DEI work can be so vast that we each need to figure out where we fit within it based on our experiences and passions. It builds off the diversity wheel elements, putting them into a broader context of how we want to participate in or lead DEI work.

The exercise is simple, but the impact is profound. This is hands-down all of my clients' favorite work to do because it gives them the space to reflect on what is personally important to them and how they can use that to benefit others.

We each have a unique story that defines us. These stories are multidimensional, and they help us understand ourselves

---

[1] https://www.linkedin.com/in/robert-simmons-iii-2179957/

and each other. They also influence how we show up in the workplace. The exercise is to think about your story and why DEI is important to you. You can draw from the diversity wheel, but I encourage you to think beyond that, dig into your personal history, and recall meaningful moments from throughout your life that gave you insight or formed your opinion about something related to DEI.

Your story starts with "I am…" and should then continue with how you identify and what has shaped who you are. There is no right or wrong way to do this. Stream-of-consciousness writing works really well here.

Here is my story, as an example:

I am….
- A woman who identifies as white, female, and heterosexual
- A former single mom of two neurodiverse teenage children
- A wife to a loving, smart, funny man who loves my kids as his own
- Someone who identifies as Californian (where I was born), even though I have lived all over the US, Europe, and in South Africa, and currently live in Texas
- The daughter of conservative parents from the South, and a graduate of UC Berkeley
- The granddaughter of two loving, gracious, tough-as-nails women who lived life on their own terms when it was far from easy to do so
- A business owner and leader
- A fierce advocate for social and systemic justice
- An avid reader and lifelong learner
- An amateur photographer
- A lover of the outdoors
- A devoted friend, sister, and niece

Through this exercise, you can see far beyond the demographics into your mindset, your character, and your areas of passion. Your story may focus more on how certain experiences felt or specific words that had a big impact. The idea is to make it truly your own.

Doing this as a team exercise helps participants know and understand each other better and identify what gifts they bring to their DEI work. It can be an intimate and highly impactful activity to share with others. You will likely find these stories inspire others to think about DEI more deeply, which will generate strong commitment to the work. Keep these close at hand as you move into DEI strategy development. You will want to weave them into those discussions and your overall communications plan.

Finally, as you start your DEI journey, it is important to remember that this work is not linear. There will be twists and turns, starts and stops. That is completely fine. It does not mean the work in total needs to end; rather, you may be creating space where none existed before for people to raise concerns or ideas that you have not heard in the past. That is a good thing! Do not be discouraged by this. Instead, assume there will be a need for pauses and build in time to gather feedback and for people to offer reflections on how the work is going at different stages. This will give you great insight into how to be most effective in your overall journey.

KEY TAKEAWAYS

- DEI work requires intentionality and is not a quick-fix solution
- Diversity is much broader than race, gender, and sexual orientation
- Equity acknowledges that we are not all starting from the same place and that support is required to get everyone to a level playing field
- Inclusion puts equity into action, creating environments where everyone can feel seen, heard, and valued for who they are
- Focusing on DEI benefits employees and employers
- DEI needs to be defined specifically to your organization's mission, values, and culture, and should be named accordingly, even if that means calling the work something other than DEI
- Before you lead DEI work, you need to define what about DEI is important to you, and why, so you can inspire and motivate others to embrace the work

CHAPTER 2

TOP FIFTEEN MYTHS ABOUT DEI WORK

A few years ago, I was asked by a client who was thinking about hiring my company to come and meet with their Board as part of the vetting process. When I asked if they wanted me to address any specific concerns or issues, they said to just talk about how we would approach the work. I knew this group was very new to DEI work, so I used the time to educate them on what DEI is, how it shows up at work, and what I anticipated helping them with based on the initial conversations I had. They were a very polite group and very quiet, so it was hard to know how the meeting was going.

At the end of the meeting, I asked them for feedback and to share anything they wished I had covered that I did not. They were silent for at least a full minute. Finally, one of the board members let out a sigh and said he was so relieved after my presentation because he thought I was going to come in and tell them they needed to set quotas and use they/them pronouns. Several others then chimed in and said they felt the same way. I explained that DEI is not about quotas, that quotas are a lose-lose because they make the person who is hired or promoted feel like they were only because they fill a certain demographic, and that employees will resent that person for being hired or promoted for the same reason. They may also resent the company for having quotas in the first place. As far as pronouns, I said using they/them pronouns, just like any other pronouns, is a sign of respect for anyone who identifies that way. We could work together on a plan to provide education on that and determine the best policy.

The reason I share this story is that you never know what assumptions people are making about DEI. Some people say they hate DEI without knowing what D, E, and I stand for, let alone the concepts behind them. It is important to recognize your own assumptions when meeting with anyone on this topic and to make sure you ask questions and listen well to set a good stage for discussion.

Here are some of the most common misconceptions about DEI I have come across over the years. I share this to help you spot the myths that you may be up against in your workplace and to get you into the frame of mind on for doing your DEI work most effectively.

MY TOP FIFTEEN MYTHS ABOUT DEI WORK

1. If we recruit differently, everything will work itself out

Recruiting with the intention of bringing in a more diverse group of new hires is not, in and of itself, a bad idea. If you bring in large groups of new hires at a time, this can be an effective way to start diversifying your workforce. However, these new recruits will be looking at your tenured employees to see if they see others like themselves as a litmus test to see if employees like them can rise to the top. If they don't, you will need to have an answer as to why and what the plan is to change that.

Additionally, you will need to ensure your current employees, as well as your policies and processes, will be supportive of a different mix of new hires and will set them up for success. If your environment is not inclusive or equitable, you will see a spike in turnover among these new hires, and DEI will be blamed. The best approach is to work on equity and inclusion first and, once you're in a good place, diversify your recruiting efforts.

Remember, it takes a long time to move entry-level employees into leadership roles. Depending only on this to get your organization to a more diverse employee mix could take fifteen or more years, assuming the majority of them stay with the company and get promoted into leadership roles. That is a long time to wait.

2. If we change the formula that has always worked for us for reviews and promotions, our business will suffer

If your review and promotion processes have resulted in a diverse set of employees being promoted into senior roles, and you have strong checks and balances to ensure bias is not creeping into those processes, then you can leave them alone. If not, you really need to look at these. If there is some homogeneity at the leadership level, your workplace could benefit from a more diverse set of experiences and perspectives in roles that drive sales, client relationships, people leadership, risk mitigation, and cost management.

Odds are, you are not promoting huge amounts of your workforce at any one time, so the risk of a change here negatively impacting your business is low, as long as you are thoughtful about the change and not suddenly promoting employees simply because they meet certain diversity criteria. This is not something you should do, for three reasons:

1. It is bad for the employee because they feel like they were promoted only because of those criteria

2. There is tremendous pressure on that employee to succeed so others can follow behind them

3. Other employees may resent them getting promoted and assume they are less qualified than others for the role

Finally, updating your review and promotion processes does not need to involve a massive overhaul. You can start by spotting where bias might creep in. For example,: Do you have documented, standard expectations for each review and clear criteria for promotion? Do those criteria include objective measures as well as subjective input? Are multiple people contributing to reviews and promotion decisions? Do you have an objective party doing a review of these? Are you providing documented feedback throughout the year on how each employee progresses alongside their goals? These are all great places to start if you answered no to any of them.

3. We have a meritocracy, so we don't need DEI, or DEI will keep us from having a meritocracy

DEI is an enabler of meritocracy. They are not at odds with each other. Those who think there is tension between them often assume that focusing on DEI means employees who fit certain diversity demographics will receive preferential treatment. This is not what DEI is about. DEI is about removing barriers and making sure everyone has an opportunity to succeed and feel like they belong at their organization just as they are. Top performers will continue to rise to leadership levels. If anything, a focus on DEI that takes a hard look at processes and ensures bias is removed as much as possible will ensure meritocracy is actually in place.

4. DEI is about making compromises on the quality of our employees

Reference the third myth!

5. If we do DEI, white men will feel targeted

DEI is not anti-white male. In fact, it is not anti-anyone. It is anti-bias and anti-discrimination, which includes making sure white men are not on the receiving end of bias or discrimination. When done right, DEI ensures everyone has an opportunity to perform to their fullest potential. All of us have a role to play in being allies to those who have historically been marginalized, and this is a great way to engage white men in your DEI plans and programs. If a white man is not promoted because a nonwhite, nonmale is based on merit, then that is a fair process.

6. DEI is about quotas

DEI is not about setting quotas, for all the reasons I mentioned above. Some companies will set goals to reach over a period of time, typically in the percentage of people in leadership roles who are women, people of color, identify as LGBTQIA+, and/or are disabled. This is different than a quota, which requires an organization to fulfill that commitment. Quotas are mandates; goals are aspirations. DEI work should include goals across a wide variety of measurable areas, such as professional development, community giving, supplier diversity spending, mentoring, and more. Using DEI as a forcing mechanism to diversify your employee demographic composition will create a lot of backlash. Developing DEI programs and initiatives to ensure equitable inclusion of all employees benefits everyone and should be largely, if not fully, supported.

7. Focusing on DEI will distract employees and make our employees less productive

DEI work ultimately needs to be owned by everyone in the organization, even though it should initially be led by a senior leader and sponsored by the whole senior leadership team. The work that comes out of DEI planning can include anything from policy design to benefits, updates, training, employee resource group (ERG) formation and support, to reviewing recruiting, annual review, and promotion processes to ensure bias is kept at bay. One of the benefits of having account- ability for DEI work spread across so many people is that it keeps any one person or group (aside a named DEI leader or team) from being so consumed by the work that they cannot be productive in their role. In fact, focusing on equity and inclusion directly corre- lates with increased engagement, which makes employ- ees more productive in their roles. We have seen this time and again in corporate teams all the way down to hourly employees in distribution centers, stores, and warehouses. This is why the case for DEI work is so strong and compelling. The results have a significant impact on the top line through productivity, sales, and innovation, and the bottom line through decreased turnover.

8. **We are a small company, so we can't do anything with DEI**

Small organizations, especially those with low turn- over, often feel like they are limited in what they can do in terms of DEI work. However, there are a lot of ways for small groups, even start-ups, to incorpo- rate DEI into their workplaces. Employee benefits are a great area to review to ensure they are fully inclu- sive and meet everyone's current and potential needs. Cultural observances can be a way to engage the team in educational and fun cultural events, whether those be monthly or quarterly. Industry organizations and nonprofits are forums to expand your DEI principles outside your workplace and to team with others to have a big impact in your community. Supplier diversity is also an initiative that any organization can put in place by looking at who you spend your money with (vendors, suppliers, business partners, and more) and ensuring some portion of those are minority-owned and/or operated.

9. **DEI is a political issue, and we don't talk politics at work**

DEI has become politicized in the US in recent years but in and of itself, is not political. DEI is about putting people first, not about what political party anyone belongs to.

10. **We have a woman and a person of color on our leadership team, so we're in good shape**

If there is an "only" on your leadership team, you still have a ways to go, especially if the pipeline of successors is not diverse. Remember, recruits and employees look to the leadership team to signal whether they will have a chance of succeeding in your organization. They want to see leaders to whom they can relate to.

11. **DEI is under attack, so it must be bad**

DEI done right is not bad for anyone.

12. **We have ERGs, so we've got DEI in a good place**

Employee resource groups (ERGs), sometimes called affinity groups or business resource groups, provide wonderful opportunities for employees to find support, leadership development, advocacy, and community outreach opportunities related to that affinity.

They also offer a way for allies to support them. However, because these groups are comprised of employees across levels and functions, they do not always have the leadership authority to drive company-wide change on their own. They are an important part of your DEI work, but not a solution in and of themselves.

13. **Parts of DEI that have been banned or deemed illegal, so we can't do this work**

Yes, there are some bans on DEI in the US, but these are focused on public colleges and universities. There are a couple of elements of DEI that have been deemed illegal by the administration in office in the US at the time of publication, but those are minimal, have been challenged, and are working their way through the courts. The schools that can no longer have DEI offices (which provided important support and community for historically underrepresented minority students) still need that support. This is a great opportunity for businesses to step in and help fill that gap, which can also provide an advantage for your company when recruiting at these schools. Similarly, businesses and employees still very much need DEI, so keep at it, steering clear of quotas and programs that give preferential treatment based on diversity demographics.

14. **Our industry isn't very diverse, so this is the best we can do**

Some industries are less diverse than others, and that is a fact we have to accept as the current state. That does not mean, however, that an organization cannot strive to outpace the diversity of its industry or help recruit a more diverse population into that industry through outreach at the high school or lower level. A lot of companies are doing this exact work through their focus on STEM (science, technology, engineering, and math). This is an area to partner with other organizations on a shared goal so you can have an even greater impact.

15. We have a DEI Task Force or Committee; we've got it handled

Organizations that view DEI work as an initiative or a project, something that is done outside of day-to-day operations, are at risk of either not moving the needle in DEI or backsliding on any progress made to date. Treating this work as an initiative dulls its impact because the real work comes in the integration of DEI into the DNA of your organization. The longer it is kept separate, the more it can be treated as a nice-to-have, with no real force behind it to drive change. That means your DEI resources can be redirected at any time.

You can have a DEI Committee be effective if it functions as an internal focus group that helps identify opportunities across the organization, has senior leaders who regularly communicate with that committee, and has close ties with key internal business partners such as HR, leadership development, communications, employee relations, and procurement to get the work accomplished.

Here is a one-page summary of these myths for easy reference:

TOP 15 MYTHS ABOUT DEI

1. IF WE RECRUIT DIFFERENTLY EVERYTHING WILL WORK ITSELF OUT

WORK ON INCLUSION AND EQUITY FIRST, THEN WORK TO HIRE IN A MORE DIVERSE GROUP OF NEW EMPLOYEES ONCE YOU KNOW THEY WILL BE SET UP FOR SUCESS

4. DEI IS ABOUT MAKING COMPROMISES ON THE QUALITY OF OUR EMPLOYEES

SEE #3!

2. IF WE CHANGE THE FORMULA THAT HAS ALWAYS WORKED FOR US FOR REVIEWS AND PROMOTIONS OUR BUSINESS WILL SUFFER

IF YOUR REVIEW AND PROMOTIONS PROCESSES HAVE RESULTED IN A DIVERSE SET OF EMPLOYEES BEING PROMOTED INTO SENIOR ROLES, AND YOU HAVE STRONG CHECKS AND BALANCES TO ENSURE BIAS IS NOT CREEPING INTO THOSE PROCESSES, THEN YOU CAN LEAVE THEM ALONE. IF NOT, YOU REALLY NEED TO LOOK AT THESE.

3. WE HAVE A MERITOCRACY SO WE DON'T NEED DEI — OR DEI WILL KEEP US FROM HAVING A MERITOCRACY

DEI IS AN ENABLER OF MERITOCRACY - THEY ARE NOT AT ODDS WITH EACH OTHER. A FOCUS ON DEI THAT TAKES A HARD LOOK AT PROCESSES AND ENSURES BIAS IS REMOVED AS MUCH AS POSSIBLE WILL ENSURE A TRUE MERITOCRACY IS IN PLACE.

5. IF WE DO DEI, WHITE MEN WILL FEEL TARGETED

DEI IS NOT ANTI-WHITE MALE. IT IS ANTI-BIAS AND ANTI-DISCRIMINATION, WHICH INCLUDES MAKING SURE WHITE MEN ARE NOT ON THE RECEIVING END OF BIAS OR DISCRIMINATION.

6. DEI IS ABOUT QUOTAS

HAVING DEI BE A FORCING MECHANISM TO DIVERSIFY YOUR EMPLOYEE DEMOGRAPHIC COMPOSITION IS BAD FOR EVERYONE. DEI SHOULD FOCUS ON REMOVING BARRIERS THAT PREVENT DIVERSITY

7. FOCUSING ON DEI WILL DISTRACT EMPLOYEES AND MAKE OUR THEM LESS PRODUCTIVE

FOCUSING ON EQUITY AND INCLUSION DIRECTLY CORRELATES WITH INCREASED ENGAGEMENT, WHICH MAKES EMPLOYEES MORE PRODUCTIVE IN THEIR ROLES

8. WE ARE A SMALL COMPANY SO WE CAN'T DO ANYTHING WITH DEI

THERE ARE MANY WAYS FOR SMALL GROUPS, EVEN START-UPS, TO INCORPORATE DEI INTO THEIR WORKPLACES: CULTURAL OBSERVANCES, BENEFITS, SUPPLIER DIVERSITY, INDUSTRY WORK, AND MORE

9. DEI IS A POLITICAL ISSUE AND WE DON'T TALK POLITICS AT WORK

DEI IS ABOUT PUTTING PEOPLE FIRST, NOT WHICH POLITICAL PARTY ANYONE BELONGS TO

11. DEI IS UNDER ATTACK SO IT MUST BE BAD

DEI DONE RIGHT IS NOT BAD FOR ANYONE

10. WE HAVE A WOMAN AND A PERSON OF COLOR ON OUR LEADERSHIP TEAM, WE'RE IN GOOD SHAPE

IF THERE IS AN "ONLY" ON YOUR LEADERSHIP TEAM, YOU'VE STILL GOT A WAYS TO GO, ESPECIALLY IF THE SUCCESSION PIPELINE IS NOT DIVERSE

12. WE HAVE EMPLOYEE RESOURCE GROUPS (ERGS) SO WE'VE GOT DEI IN A GOOD PLACE

ERGS TYPICALLY DON'T HAVE THE LEADERSHIP AUTHORITY TO DRIVE COMPANY-WIDE CHANGE ON THEIR OWN. THEY ARE AN IMPORTANT PART OF DEI BUT NOT A SOLUTION IN AND OF THEMSELVES

13. PARTS OF DEI HAVE BEEN BANNED OR DEEMED ILLEGAL, SO WE CAN'T DO THIS WORK

THERE ARE SOME BANS ON DEI, BUT THESE ARE FOCUSED ON PUBLIC COLLEGES AND UNIVERSITIES. A FEW ASPECTS OF DEI HAVE BEEN DEEMED ILLEGAL AND ARE BEING CHALLENGED IN THE COURTS. KEEP WORKING AT WHAT IS LEGAL.

14. OUR INDUSTRY ISN'T VERY DIVERSE SO THIS IS THE BEST WE CAN DO

SOME INDUSTRIES LACK SIGNIFICANT DIVERSITY, BUT YOU CAN STILL AIM TO OUTPACE YOUR INDUSTRY AND HELP RECRUIT A MORE DIVERSE POPULATION INTO IT FROM HIGH SCHOOL

15. WE HAVE A DEI TASK FORCE OR COMMITTEE, WE'VE GOT IT HANDLED

ORGANIZATIONS THAT VIEW DEI WORK AS AN INITIATIVE OR A PROJECT OUTSIDE OF DAY-TO-DAY OPERATIONS ARE AT RISK OF NOT MOVING THE NEEDLE IN DEI IN A SIGNIFICANT WAY

Scan this QR code to access a digital version of the
Top 15 Myths About DEI:

Password: DoDEIRight

KEY TAKEAWAYS

There are a lot of myths about DEI. Don't assume that someone's perception of DEI is based on factual or accurate information. Being prepared to dig deeper into conversations about what DEI is and is not will set your organization up for success.

CHAPTER 3

THE EQUITY AT WORK™ DEI MATURITY MODEL & IMPACT FRAMEWORK

In early 2022, I got a phone call from a former colleague, who is now working at an innovative global Fortune 100 company. She was in a role within the supply chain division, charged with opening new facilities all over the US to distribute their product to retailers and directly to consumers. She said, "I'm standing up a new distribution center, and we've decided we want it to be a DEI benchmark facility." I thought that was amazing and congratulated her for taking such a bold stance, especially in a space that is predominantly staffed with hourly employees. She went on to say, "The thing is, none of us knows what that means. Can you help us figure that out and then show us how to do it?"

Are you kidding?! Yes!!

Three years later, we are still working together across several sites in their network, continuing to embed DEI into all the ways of working in those buildings, across the organization, and out in their communities. Through that work, and work with other clients, I developed a model to show the evolution of DEI from an HR compliance activity to a robust program that could fundamentally change how employers and employees work together. And so was born the Equity At Work™ DEI Maturity Model.

The Equity At Work™ DEI Maturity Model is a framework any organization can use to think through its DEI strategy and roadmap, and how the work can evolve. It outlines all the elements that go into setting a strong foundation for DEI in your organization, how you evolve to embed it into your company's DNA, and then how you move into continuous improvement while expanding your principles and impact outside your organization. It shows you what to include, how to sequence your work, and what cultural elements need to be in place for the work to be successful and to move from one phase to the next.

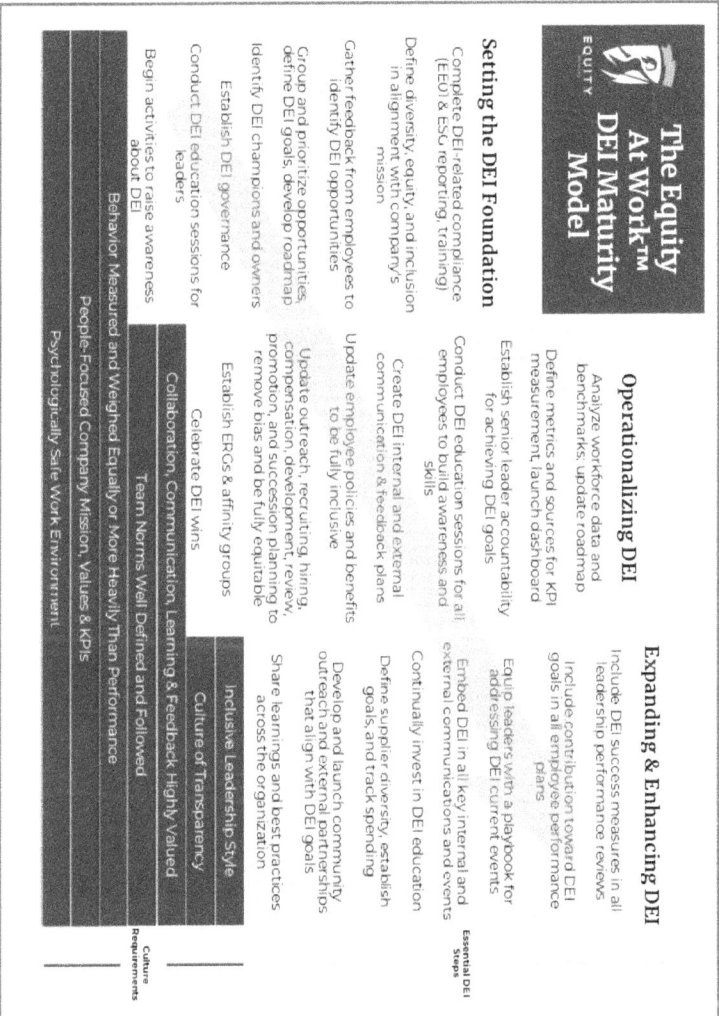

The Equity At Work™ DEI Maturity Model

Essential DEI Steps

Setting the DEI Foundation
- Complete DEI-related compliance (EEO) & ESG reporting, training)
- Define diversity, equity, and inclusion in alignment with company's mission
- Gather feedback from employees to identify DEI opportunities
- Group and prioritize opportunities, define DEI goals, develop roadmap
- Identify DEI champions and owners
- Conduct DEI education sessions for leaders
- Begin activities to raise awareness about DEI

Operationalizing DEI
- Analyze workforce data and benchmarks, update roadmap
- Define metrics and sources for KPI measurement, launch dashboard
- Establish senior leader accountability for achieving DEI goals
- Conduct DEI education sessions for all employees to build awareness and skills
- Create DEI internal and external communication & feedback plans
- Update employee policies and benefits to be fully inclusive
- Update outreach, recruiting, hiring, compensation, development, review, promotion, and succession planning to remove bias and be fully equitable

Expanding & Enhancing DEI
- Include DEI success measures in all leadership performance reviews
- Include contribution toward DEI goals in all employee performance plans
- Equip leaders with a playbook for addressing DEI current events
- Embed DEI in all key internal and external communications and events
- Continually invest in DEI education
- Define supplier diversity, establish goals, and track spending
- Develop and launch community outreach and external partnerships that align with DEI goals
- Share learnings and best practices across the organization

Culture Requirements
- Establish DEI governance
- Establish ERGs & affinity groups
- Inclusive Leadership Style
- Celebrate DEI wins
- Culture of Transparency
- Collaboration, Communication, Learning & Feedback Highly Valued
- Behavior Measured and Weighed Equally or More Heavily Than Performance
- Team Norms Well Defined and Followed
- People-Focused Company Mission, Values & KPIs
- Psychologically Safe Work Environment

Scan the QR code to access a digital version
of The Equity At Work™ DEI Maturity Model:

Password: DoDEIRight

Oftentimes, organizations launch DEI through a scattershot approach, starting multiple efforts without grounding them in a plan or a specific desired outcome. If you are looking to make a major change in your organization, you run the risk of people feeling like they are spinning their wheels with this approach. Without stated goals and a tracking mechanism for achievements you are making along the way to reaching your goals, you put your work at risk of losing resources and budget.

This is where the Equity At Work™ DEI Maturity Model can help you. It creates a framework for methodically working through the key steps of DEI work, whether you have a singular goal, like my former firm's, of advancing more women into senior leader roles, or are looking to affect more widespread change, such as company-wide education; overhauling policies, processes, and benefits to be fully equitable and inclusive; or establishing internal and external communications platforms for your stance on DEI issues and cultural observances.

This model does not aim to tell you that you must stay in one phase completely before starting efforts in the next. Instead, it shows you what you should have in good shape before moving fully into the next phase. For example, many organizations will do company-wide training (part of Operationalizing DEI) before they have defined their DEI goals and established governance. This can work, especially if that training is part of onboarding or ongoing people-manager training, because those are natural times to teach expected behaviors and skills.

If you are starting at step 1, this model will give you a good blueprint for how to proceed. My number one piece of guidance is to develop your DEI strategy and roadmap in a way that aligns with and enhances your culture. That includes how quickly you tackle the items in here. If you are a slow-and-steady organization, this is not the time to suddenly go fast. It will cause too much disruption. There is a time and place to shake things up. If you feel like you are going to encounter resistance with this work, do not force it. Develop an approach that will work with your organization's culture to drive progress.

Even if you are currently doing a little bit of work in each phase, I do not recommend jumping to do all of the items listed in Operationalizing DEI before you have set the foundation effectively and ensured you have the cultural requirements in place. I also strongly recommend shoring up everything in the middle phase before moving to Expanding & Enhancing. Otherwise, you risk layering initiatives onto a cracked cultural foundation, which will exacerbate existing problems and bring them to the surface. Getting them to the surface is good because then they can be addressed. However, that needs to be done before you invest a lot of time and effort into your DEI work, or DEI will be incorrectly blamed and/or the investment you have made in your DEI work will go to waste.

You may be surprised that the external work is held for the final phase. This is not a hard-and-fast rule, but I recommend clients get their houses in order before focusing on external work. However, you may be in an industry that is very focused on DEI and offers opportunities to collaborate with partners to have a big impact on your community, universities, or industry organizations. If so, jump in!

Another element I've developed to go hand in hand with the Equity At Work™ DEI Maturity Model is the Equity At Work™ DEI Impact Framework. This is a framework for you to plot the DEI activities you want to pursue based on the impact they can have. The x-axis spans individual impact to enterprise-wide impact, while the y-axis spans low to high financial impact. The axes are the steady pieces here; you can plot any DEI activity you are considering or planning on the framework.

The purpose of this framework is to help you understand the trade-offs between DEI initiatives and to help you prioritize what you go after based on your desired impact.

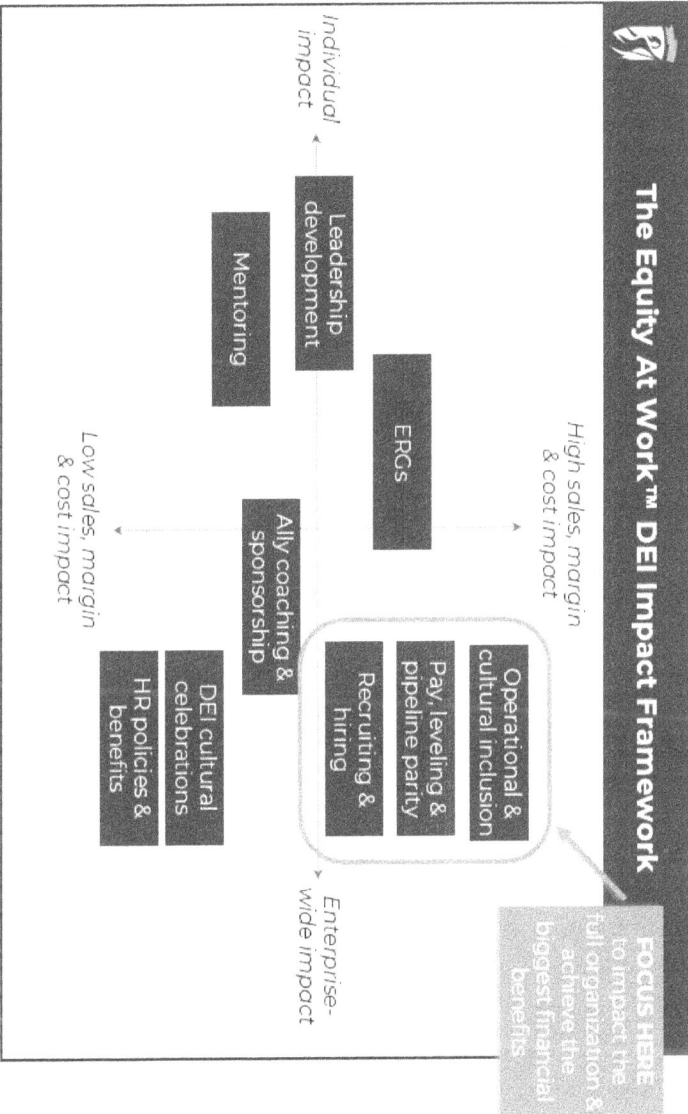

EXAMPLE – LARGE ORGANIZATION:

The Equity At Work™ DEI Impact Framework

Individual impact

Leadership development

Mentoring

ERGs

High sales, margin & cost impact

Ally coaching & sponsorship

Low sales, margin & cost impact

Operational & cultural inclusion

Pay, leveling & pipeline parity

Recruiting & hiring

DEI cultural celebrations

HR policies & benefits

Enterprise-wide impact

FOCUS HERE to impact the full organization & achieve the biggest financial benefits

Scan the QR code to access a digital version of
The Equity At Work™ DEI Impact Framework:

Password: DoDEIRight

The example above shows how a large organization is thinking about its DEI work. If they wanted to move the needle for a small group of employees, let's say developing a more robust pipeline to leadership for employees from disadvantaged backgrounds, they could prioritize leadership development and mentoring within their roadmap. This has a pretty neutral financial impact since they are focusing on a small group within a large organization. However, if they wanted to focus on ensuring the entire organization has a strong sense of inclusion and that they are recruiting, hiring, compensating, and promoting all employees fairly, they would focus on the upper-right quadrant. That area of focus also has a higher financial return, as that work results in lower turnover, higher engagement, higher productivity, and greater innovation.

As you build your own version of the Equity At Work™ DEI Impact Framework, review where your activities are concentrated, the breadth of your impact (individual to enterprise-wide), and the degree of financial impact associated with each:

- Does this match what you are looking to achieve?
- Are there any key constituents left out that you need to consider or add in?
- Are there any other changes you need to make?

I recommend using this as a living document. It is a great tool for socializing what you want to achieve with leaders, and it is something you can update yearly as you get different elements in place.

There is no one way to build this framework. It is meant to be totally customized to your organization's interests and priorities. A smaller organization may include some external DEI activities in its model because that is the avenue for them to have the biggest impact. For example, my team and I work with several financial services organizations that have small headcounts and low turnover but manage significant investments and are heavy hitters in their industries. There typically are not enough employees to have robust ERG programs or greatly impact their diversity at different levels through recruiting and promotions, but they can work to make their processes equitable, have organization-wide cultural celebrations, focus leadership development on increasing inclusion, and lead major industry initiatives.

I recognize this is a lot to think through! I'll walk you through each of the phases in the Equity At Work™ DEI Maturity Model step by step in the following chapters and guide you on how to determine the impact you want to have. Think of these two frameworks as tools in your DEI toolbelt to help you build your DEI roadmap and stay focused on the impact you want to have.

KEY TAKEAWAYS

- There are phases to DEI work, from foundational to continuous improvement

- While you do not need to stay fully in one phase at a time, it is important to shore up one phase before fully moving into the next

- Each phase has cultural dependencies that must be in place for your DEI efforts to work

- As you think about how the Equity At Work™ DEI Maturity Model applies to your organization, consider the impact you are looking to have

- Developing your own DEI Impact Model will keep you clear on your priorities and help you stay focused on making an impact through your work

CHAPTER 4

SETTING THE FOUNDATION

In the Introduction, I shared the challenge that I, and so many other women at the time, faced when trying to get promoted to partner at my former consulting firm. After being rejected the first time I was up for promotion because my maternity leave interrupted my required three-year consistent sales and delivery performance, I was promoted the second time around, and as soon as I was over that hurdle, I was determined to change our process. I had seen so many talented women get stuck or leave the firm over the ten years I had been there, and our firm, employees, and clients were suffering as a result. But I was in an organization that felt it had figured out the "magic formula" for getting the "right" people to the partner level. How could I really change that?

Fortunately, I worked with wonderful women, even if there were few of us at any particular level or any location across the US. We had a connection and wanted to create ways to help each other. While it is more common now for women to support each other at work, back in the early 2000s, women still typically felt only one or two of us would ever have a chance to get promoted to a senior-level role, so we viewed each other as competition. Fortunately, we did not have a limit to how many people we could have at any one level at a time at this firm, so that took the competitive feeling out of the equation. We started holding a series of conference calls for the women to connect with each other (this was back before Zoom, and video calls were still very rare), and we decided to launch our first women's network. This enabled us to have a sense of community, to have a forum to discuss the issues that were the most challenging for us, and to identify what we wanted to ask the firm to change.

It did not feel completely safe for us to create the group at first, as we were worried about creating division between ourselves and the rest of the firm by doing so. But ultimately, the need for connection and support was so strong that we charged ahead and did it. Those of us who were more senior spent a lot of time myth-busting with our male counterparts and explaining the purpose of the group: no, we were not meeting to bash the men or try to figure out how to overthrow the patriarchy. Instead, we were trying to support each other and make our firm a place where everyone had an opportunity to be a great performer, thrive, and get promoted, even if they took a less traditional path to get there or came from a different background than current and historical leaders.

We made some progress, but really it was largely in the low-hanging-fruit department for some time. We got a budget and were able to bring in a speaker. We started a book club, and, most importantly, we started creating connections and lines of communication for women across offices and roles who we would not otherwise have met or worked with.

There was one thing that turned the tide for us, and this was what ultimately led me to this work and to launching a business to help organizations get this right. After several years of the group being in place, we were still not moving the needle on getting more women to the partner level. Any challenge to that generated a response that tried to blame a woman not getting promoted on a personal situation rather than something systemic. My gut told me data would help us see the problem more clearly. Rather than go through approvals to get access to HR data, I pulled out an organization chart and manually tallied up the men and women by level across the firm. I created one slide that showed the ratio of men to women at each level.

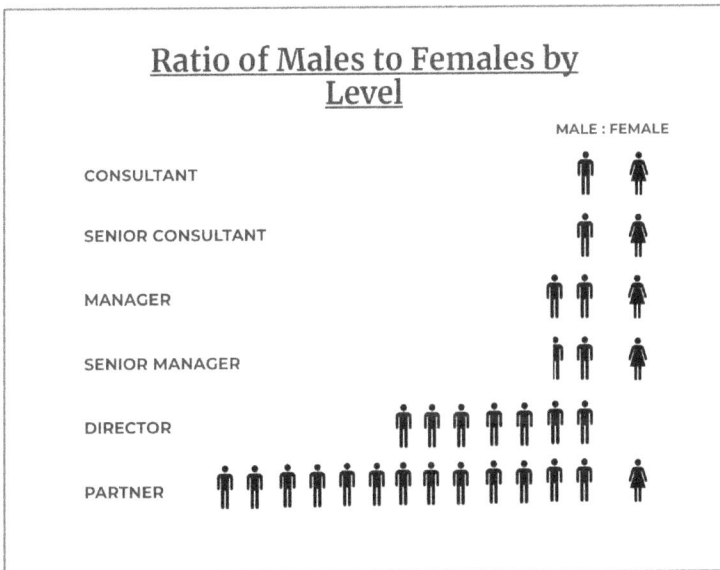

Ratio of Males to Females by Level

MALE : FEMALE

CONSULTANT	
SENIOR CONSULTANT	
MANAGER	
SENIOR MANAGER	
DIRECTOR	
PARTNER	

When I shared this with our leadership team, they were silent. Then our head of North America said, "This is not who we are as a firm. We have to do better." With that, we got huge buy-in to look at our processes and policies with a more inclusive and equitable lens.

Over time, this created a movement, one that not only benefitted women but also benefited anyone who wasn't the traditional mold for that firm. We had a work environment that became welcoming and supportive of LGBTQIA+ employees, employees of color, single parents, fathers who wanted schedule flexibility, caretakers of aging parents, people who wanted to take a sabbatical, and more. Our retention improved drastically, our engagement went up, and we promoted more women, people of color, and LGBTQIA+ employees into senior roles, including partner. And we had our most profitable years on record once we had this in place. Long before the business case for DEI work was researched, we proved it ourselves.

We did not start this work as an organized, strategic initiative. It began much more grassroots, and we came together as a small group within our organization to try to remedy a problem. The turning point was that we moved from trying to figure out the problem as individual women to trying to solve it as an ERG, to mobilizing our senior leaders and the firm to tackle it as a strategic initiative. That was when real change happened.

Having clarity on your vision, in our case, that we wanted more women in every role at our firm, including the most senior role, is key to mobilizing change. From there, you can develop a strategy and a plan or roadmap to make the change happen. Our goal required us to look at every step of the employee lifecycle to strip bias out and create more than one path to promotion. If we were not recruiting, developing, and advancing women equitably to men, we couldn't get women to fill a meaningful number of the most senior-level roles. These became the key steps on our roadmap, and we measured promotion rates as we worked to get these changes in place to make sure we were getting the results we wanted. That created visibility and accountability for the change.

Let's do a deeper dive into the first phase of the model, Setting the DEI Foundation.

Setting the DEI Foundation

Complete DEI-related compliance
(EEO1 & ESG reporting, training)

Define diversity, equity, and inclusion
in alignment with company's mission

Gather feedback from employees to
identify DEI opportunities

Group and prioritize opportunities,
define DEI goals, develop roadmap

Essential DEI Steps

Identify DEI champions and owners

Establish DEI governance

Conduct DEI education sessions for
leaders

Begin activities to raise awareness
about DEI

Behavior Measured and Weighed
Equally or More Heavily Than
Performance

People-Focused Company Mission,
Values & KPIs

Culture Requirements

Psychologically Safe Work
Environment

COMPLETE DEI-RELATED COMPLIANCE (EEO1 & ESG REPORTING, TRAINING)

EEO-1 reporting refers to the US government's Equal Employment Opportunity Commission (EEOC)[2] requirement that employers with fifty or more employees self-report a census with any data captured about the protected classes. That reporting also includes a pay equity study to demonstrate equal pay for equal work within your organization. Large firms typically outsource the pay equity piece to an employment attorney or other specialist who can provide benchmark data and be an outside, objective party to validate that you are providing equal pay for equal work.

The EEOC is also the body that reviews any claims of harassment or discrimination filed by employees. The EEOC issued updated guidelines in April 2024[3] to address how harassment based on race, color, religion, sex (including pregnancy, childbirth, or related medical conditions; sexual orientation; and gender identity), national origin, age, disability, or genetic information is defined and how liability is determined.

The EEOC provides guidelines with over seventy examples. All of these should be part of your workplace policies and supporting education and coaching on dos and don'ts as part of your DEI work so everyone can feel safe at work and be able to contribute as their full, authentic selves.

Below are some of the key takeaways, sourced directly from the EEOC. EEOC laws and guidance evolve over time, so be sure to visit their website[4] for the most up-to-date information.

---

[2] https://www.eeoc.gov/
[3] https://www.eeoc.gov/laws/guidance/enforcement-guidance-harassment-workplace
[4] https://www.eeoc.gov/

- Race: use of racial epithets, offensive comments, and stereotypes as well as harassment based on traits or characteristics linked to an individual's race, including name, cultural dress, accent, manner of speech, and physical and appearance standards such as hairstyles and textures

- Color: harassment based on an individual's pigmentation, complexion, skin shade, or tone

- National origin: use of ethnic epithets; derogatory comments about a person's nationality; stereotypes; traits; physical and linguistic characteristics, including diet, attire, and accent

- Religion: use of religious epithets; offensive comments about an individual's religion or lack of religious belief, religious practices or dress, or religious accommodation, and explicitly or implicitly coercing employees to engage in religious practices at work

- Sex (includes pregnancy, childbirth, and related medical conditions; sexual orientation; gender identity): unwanted conduct expressing sexual attraction or involving sexual activity, sexual attention or coercion, sexual violence, discussing or displaying visual depictions of sex acts or sexual remarks; lactation; using or not using contraception; deciding to have or not have an abortion; how sexual orientation or gender identity is expressed including epithets, outing an individual, intentional use of a name or pronoun inconsistent with the individual's known gender identity, or denial of access to a bathroom or other sex-segregated facility consistent with the individual's gender identity

- Age: harassment of employees over forty years of age, including those based on negative perceptions or stereotypes about older workers

- Disability: includes physical and mental disability stereo-types, traits, and characteristics; harassment based on a request for and/or receipt of accommodation; harass-ment because of an impairment even if it is not a dis-ability; harassment based on the disability of someone, with whom an individual is associated

- Genetic information: harassment based on an individ-ual's or family member's genetic test or medical history

ESG reporting is the Environmental, Social, and Gover-nance reporting identified by the US Securities and Exchange Commission (SEC) for public companies in the US[5]. DEI work is in the "S" in ESG. These requirements are constantly chang-ing, so go to SEC.gov for the most up-to-date information.

In 2023, the European Union (EU) had a number of requirements come into effect that have a direct impact on US businesses[67]. All public EU companies are required to disclose this information. While these directives originate in the EU, as of the time of publication, any public US company with an office or subsidiary business in the EU consisting of 500 or more employees and 150 million Euros or more in revenue must comply. Be sure to visit the European Commission's

---

[5] https://www.sec.gov/

[6] https://finance.ec.europa.eu/capital-markets-union-and-financial-markets/company-reporting-and-auditing/company-reporting/corporate-sustainability-reporting_en

[7]https://www.consilium.europa.eu/en/press/press-releases/2023/12/14/corporate-sustainability-due-diligence-council-and-parliament-strike-deal-to-protect-environment-and-human-rights/#:~:text=The%20due%20diligence%20directive%20lays,the%20downstream%20activities%2C%20such%20as

Corporate Sustainability Reporting website for the most up-to-date information.[8]

Here are the two primary divisions of the EU directives relevant to DEI and how you can prepare as a US company:

1. Include activities directly owned by your organization
   - Reporting needs to include activities directly owned by the organization, as well as those the organization contributes to and those that are linked to its value chain:
     - ○ This means that your compliance efforts should expand well beyond the four walls of your business out into all aspects of your supply chain, operating partners, and areas of business impact.
       - ❏ Make sure any subcontractors, vendors, and key business partners, as well as community, nonprofit, and academic institutions that are partners or recipients of funding, are in scope.
   - Here are some steps you can take to prepare your reporting:
     - ○ Define how your DEI vision and desired outcomes tie to your value chain and out into the communities you operate in.
     - ○ Develop goals and define metrics to track and communicate progress in these areas.

---

[8] https://finance.ec.europa.eu/capital-markets-union-and-financial-markets/company-reporting-and-auditing/company-reporting/corporate-sustainability-reporting_en

- ○ Develop supplier diversity programs that attract, recruit, onboard, and support business partners from historically marginalized communities.
  - ❏ There are a number of certification councils that validate that owners and operators are women, racial minorities, LGBTQIA+, veterans, and/or disabled.
  - ❏ These councils can be excellent sources of suppliers, education, and other programming to help you get started and set your suppliers up for success.
- ○ Define the impact you want to have in your communities and identify partners who can help you achieve those goals.
  - ❏ These can include academic institutions, nonprofits, Chambers of Commerce, and more.

1. Include all relevant data
   - ● Reporting should include data on pay equity, professional development, unionization, board participation and composition, and incidents of discrimination across all demographics.
     - ○ This means that, in total and by all demographics mandated by each country, reporting needs to include:
       - ❏ Equal pay for work of equal value
       - ❏ Executive-to-worker pay ratios
       - ❏ Proportion and demographics of employees participating in training and skill development

❏ Existence of unions and proportion of employees covered

❏ Participation of employees on administrative and advisory boards

❏ Reported incidents of discrimination

❏ Specifically for gender, reporting should include gender equality work and metrics, gender diversity at top management, and number of members of the underrepresented sex on boards

❏ Specifically for disabled employees, reporting should include accessibility measures designed to protect rights of people with disabilities

Other areas to include are your company's policies on human rights (such as forced labor and child labor), working conditions, equal opportunities for all, nondiscrimination, diversity and inclusion, collective bargaining, impact on people and human health, and social partner involvement. All of this information must be disclosed as part of ESG reporting and validated by a third party.

DEFINE DIVERSITY, EQUITY, AND INCLUSION IN ALIGNMENT WITH YOUR COMPANY'S MISSION

Just as I defined diversity, equity, and inclusion in Chapter One, you should define what these terms mean in your organization. That may lead you to use different words for these concepts, and if that helps them align better with your mission and culture, you should absolutely do that. DEI work needs to align with, improve, and enhance your culture, not function outside of it.

This is an important step to spend time on and ensure your senior leadership team is aligned with each other moving forward. I often have organizations define not just the terms but how an employee—or a cross-section of employees—would experience each of them in their regular work experience as a way to make this exercise less academic. For some, diversity is focused specifically on gender and race, while others open the diversity aperture much wider. Some include diversity of thought and experience in here; others focus more on demographic dimensions. There is a wide variance in how companies define equity and inclusion as well. Some will bring belonging and engagement into the definitions here. The right approach is to get this in the language and sentiment of your organization's culture and show how it helps your company live out its mission.

GATHER FEEDBACK FROM EMPLOYEES TO IDENTIFY DEI OPPORTUNITIES

DO NOT SKIP THIS! Your employees will have a lot of ideas on how to make their work environments more diverse, equitable, and inclusive. Including them in the early stages sends a powerful message about how much you value their perspective and input. You will generate a ton of goodwill by reaching out to employees and providing multiple ways for them to provide input, so each person can do so in the way they feel most comfortable.

Many leadership teams, especially in hierarchical organizations, feel they need to define their plans for DEI first and then communicate down what will be done for DEI work. This is the time to flip that concept on its head and use an inclusive process. Listen to your employees and based on their input, determine as leaders how you want to move forward. Be sure to thank your employees for their input and share back what you heard, what you will act on both now and in the future, anything you will not act on and why, and what the plan and general timing are going forward. Your plans and timetable do not need to be highly specific at this stage. This is about appreciating your employees' input and demonstrating to them that you are taking it seriously. That will go a long way in building trust and setting the tone of an inclusive culture.

My team and I leverage a lot of different methods and tools to gather input, including:

- Site visits to each location
- One-on-one meetings
- Focus groups
- Small cohort meetings of peers
- Office hours for employees to drop in confidentially
- Engagement surveys (typically once per year)
- Pulse surveys (spot checks on a small number of issues) throughout the year
- Employee relations data and reports
- Exit interview feedback
- Outreach to company alumni
- Glassdoor and other online employee feedback forums

Based on the size and structure of your organization, you will need to determine the best ways to gather input. Many employees are skeptical that surveys claiming to be confidential really are, so if you are using surveys, be sure to demonstrate how you are ensuring privacy and confidentiality. Using an outside party for this step can put employees' minds at ease on this point.

It is highly likely that you will uncover some human resources-related issues through this exercise. If that is the case, be sure to share them with your HR team, discuss the follow-up plan, and include that in your feedback on what you heard. It is important to tackle those issues as they come up.

GROUP AND PRIORITIZE OPPORTUNITIES, DEFINE DEI GOALS, DEVELOP ROADMAP

Now that you have input from your employees, you will want to organize and review it with your leadership team. Based on this input, plus their perspectives and any knowledge they have of what competitors or other organizations are doing, the leadership team can determine the goals of your DEI work and prioritize actions accordingly.

This is a framework we use at Equity At Work™ to help our clients brainstorm their DEI goals:

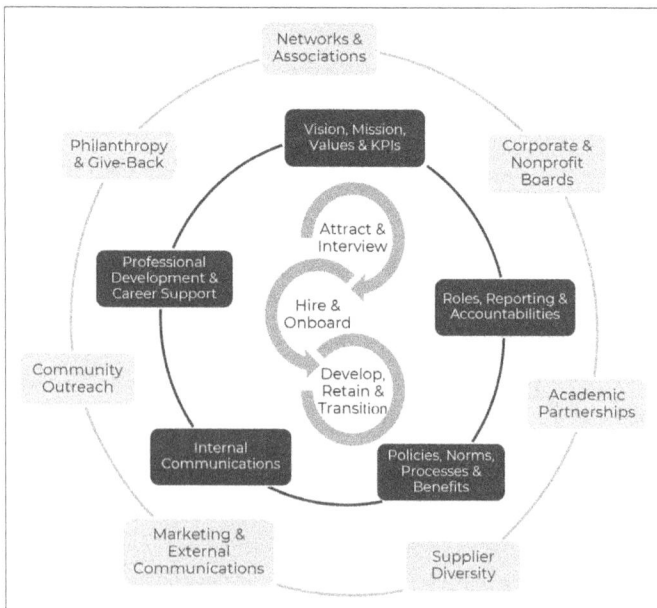

The center circles include all the steps of the employee life-cycle that DEI should touch. The dark boxes in the middle are the key organizational areas where DEI needs to be incorporated. Finally, the outer areas highlight where you can extend your DEI work externally. The best practice is to integrate DEI into all the ways you interact with your employees, your business model, and your external community, so you want to think through all three realms when determining your DEI goals.

It is also important to think through what may be a symptom versus a root cause when you determine your goals. If you only focus on the symptom, you may fix that but have the issue pop up in a different way elsewhere. A great exercise to use here is to go through the "Five Whys" for any goal you identify. To use this approach, start with a problem statement and then ask why that problem exists. Once you have that answer, ask why again, and continue until you have five "why" questions answered.

Here is an example:

PROBLEM: WE HAVE VERY FEW WOMEN IN SENIOR LEADERSHIP ROLES

- Why? Because we do not have any women in the internal pipeline for these roles
- Why? Because mid-management women tend to leave
- Why? Because we have rigid promotion criteria and timing, and a strict up-or-out policy
- Why? Because that's how we have always done things
- Why? Because that is what worked when the company was founded

As you can see, this approach identifies multiple areas to explore to solve the problem. It is also easy to imagine multiple answers to the "why" questions. If this happens, list them all and continue down the "why" path for each one.

This is a terrific exercise to do as a group, whether it be within an ERG, with a meeting of all ERG leaders, in a DEI Committee, in a Culture Council meeting, or as some other DEI-related working or project team. The more inclusive the process, the better it will work, because you will have a wider representation of employees answering the "whys" and brainstorming potential solutions.

Finally, be sure to follow the "SMART" model when setting your goals—Specific, Measurable, Achievable, Realistic, and Time-bound. Another piece of advice I share with clients on this step is to complete the sentence "We will know we have achieved this goal when _____." Being diligent here will give you the best chance of meeting your goals.

One of Equity At Work™'s clients wanted to make the commitment personal at the leadership level, using this template for leaders to complete and then check back in on with each other:

Personal Commitment Statement

I will begin _____ (steps/activities)

in the next _____ (# months)

to mitigate systemic bias at our company.

This will be done _____ (frequency).

My accountability partner is _____ (name)

and we will review progress every _____ (frequency).

I will know I have succeeded

when I see _____ (impact),

which I expect to take _____ (# weeks/months/years)

to achieve.

Many of our clients summarize their goals in statements or commitments they make to their organizations. This can be a great way to codify what you intend to achieve through your DEI work. Here is one example:

Our Diversity, Equity, and Inclusion Commitment

This will be a place where every person, regardless of role, background, or time with the company, matters and is respected as much for who they are as for their contribution.

We will set a new standard for going beyond policy and process into fully living out our diversity, equity, and inclusion goals in order to deliver excellence while establishing a best-in-class approach for the industry.

We will demonstrate our commitment to diversity, equity, and inclusion by incorporating it into our behaviors, goals, KPIs, operations, education, and the models for partnership and community support we create.

Employees at every level will embody the diversity of the community, as will our suppliers, service providers, and business partners. We will support and grow our employees so they are provided opportunities to develop to their full potential. We will create a safe space for everyone to have a voice in how we can do better. Finally, we will be transparent in our progress, applying a continuous learning approach and holding ourselves accountable for our results.

Once you have defined your goals, you can begin to identify the work needed to achieve those goals and create a roadmap or timeline for the work. At this phase, it will be more of a straw man than a fully developed roadmap since you still need to identify who will fill critical roles. But it is a great time to start visualizing what you want to pursue. Later work on building your business case will also help you define your roadmap more specifically.

Here is an example roadmap for a client in the early stages of their DEI journey:

Roadmap: Top 10 DEI Priorities

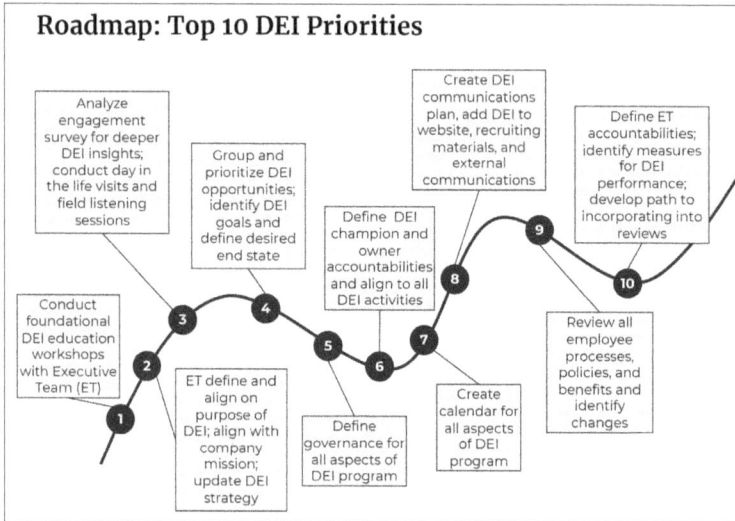

This roadmap has not addressed timing or ownership yet; rather, it focuses on prioritizing the key steps needed to move forward with their DEI work at a high level. From here, the team developed more details for each step, including relative priority levels and dependencies.

Here is an extract of the Setting the DEI Foundation steps as an example:

Setting the DEI Foundation: Findings & Recommendations

MATURITY MODEL ACTIVITY	OBSERVATIONS	RECOMMENDATION	PRIORITY	ROADMAP #
Conduct DEI education sessions for leaders	• Completed in past to varying effectiveness	• Conduct workshops to create common language for DEI and educate on how to create equitable and inclusive environments	High	1
Define diversity, equity and inclusion in alignment with company mission	• D&I strategy and definition developed but needs refresh	• Update strategy to define purpose of DEI and alignment with mission, values, etc. • Ensure full ET commitment	High	2
Gather feedback from employees to identify DEI opportunities	• Engagement survey has high scores and participation • Female roundtable conducted	• Variances in engagement survey responses across regions and lines of reporting needs deeper dive • ET and DEI team conduct "day in the life" listening sessions in the field	High	3
Group and prioritize opportunities, define goals	• Defined as part of 2020 strategy	• Update to align with purpose of DEI • Identify goals and desired end state	High	4
Establish DEI governance	• Not formally in place	• Define for all aspects of DEI program	High	5
Identify DEI champions & owners	• Sponsors for DEI events in place	• DEI Champion role not fully defined or formalized across all DEI initiatives	Medium	6
Begin activities to raise awareness about DEI	• DEI observances and cultural events underway, first ERG launched	• Create calendar with ongoing observances, activities, and events	Medium	7
Complete DEI-related compliance	• EEO1 in place today • ESG not required because not public company	• Launch self ID reporting on LGBTQ+, veteran, and disabled employees • Develop regular DEI communications to raise awareness and maintain momentum with all stakeholders	Medium	8

The observations column captures any work done to date so the team can have clarity on what has been tried before, what is in place, and what still needs to be done. The recommendations column provides more detail on what is needed for each step, and then the priority ratings help the team sort the work. From here, we incorporated any intersection with other strategic initiatives, added timing and owners, and created a more robust project plan for the work.

Here is an example of a time-bound roadmap, which can also be used as a tool to report progress monthly:

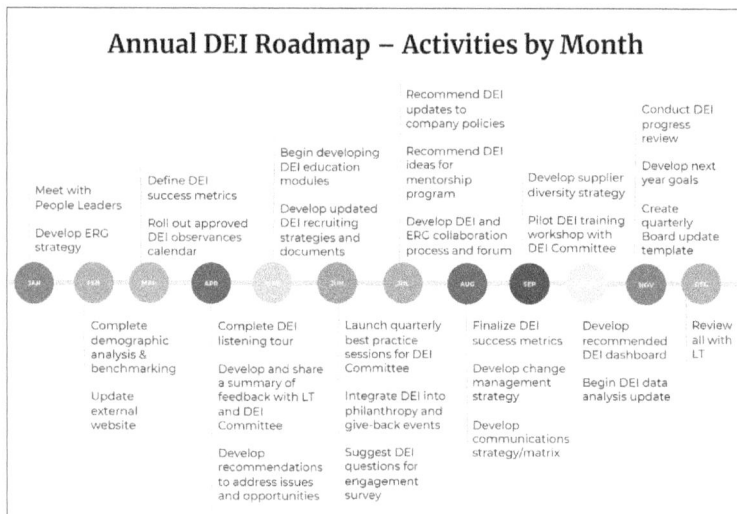

Annual DEI Roadmap – Activities by Month

	JAN	FEB	MAR	APR	MAY	JUN	JUL	AUG	SEP	OCT	NOV	DEC

Above the line:

- JAN: Meet with People Leaders; Develop ERG strategy
- FEB: Define DEI success metrics; Roll out approved DEI observances calendar
- MAR: Begin developing DEI education modules; Develop updated DEI recruiting strategies and documents
- MAY: Recommend DEI updates to company policies; Recommend DEI ideas for mentorship program; Develop DEI and ERC collaboration process and forum
- AUG: Develop supplier diversity strategy
- SEP: Pilot DEI training workshop with DEI Committee
- OCT: Conduct DEI progress review; Develop next year goals; Create quarterly Board update template

Below the line:

- FEB: Complete demographic analysis & benchmarking; Update external website
- APR: Complete DEI listening tour; Develop and share a summary of feedback with LT and DEI Committee; Develop recommendations to address issues and opportunities
- JUN: Launch quarterly best practice sessions for DEI Committee; Integrate DEI into philanthropy and give-back events; Suggest DEI questions for engagement survey
- AUG: Finalize DEI success metrics; Develop change management strategy; Develop communications strategy/matrix
- OCT: Develop recommended DEI dashboard; Begin DEI data analysis update
- DEC: Review all with LT

You will iterate on this, ultimately developing a robust plan as you work through additional steps in the Equity At Work™ Maturity Model.

IDENTIFY DEI CHAMPIONS AND OWNERS

Your CEO needs to lead from the front on this work, role-modeling behaviors and actions that she/he/they want others to follow. The CEO is your ultimate champion and owner. However, other champions and owners need to be spread out across your organization so everyone is marching toward the same goals.

Champions, who may also be called sponsors, should be people leaders who can check in on progress, raise issues with senior leaders, remove barriers, and address day-to-day needs that come up. They are the ones who are steadfast support-ers of DEI work, willing to engage with people who have concerns or push back while standing strong with everyone charged with doing the DEI work.

I will never forget meeting with a prominent female CEO who spoke publicly about family support policies, the impor-tance of creating different paths to the top, and work/life bal-ance. She presented herself as the ultimate Champion for DEI work. Less than ten minutes later, she told me privately about how she arranged 24/7 childcare so that she never had to be home with her children and shared her belief that the traditional career path is the only path to success. This undermined every speech and PR effort she led around equity in the workplace. It was clear she had been coached about her public persona and embraced it even though it was opposed to how she operated. As soon as she opened up to me, I knew her words were purely performative. Champions need to walk the walk, not just talk the talk. "Do as I say, not as I do" does not work here.

Owners are the ones who are accountable for the work being completed. Depending on what your focus areas are, you may have owners in communications, human resources, inves-tor relations, and/or business analytics, as well as people in roles such as ERG leaders and DEI Committee Members. Owners can delegate responsibilities but are ultimately accountable for reporting progress to the leadership team. Depending on your culture and operating structure, updates may first go through the Chief People Officer or Chief DEI Officer before reaching the senior team, or they may go directly to leadership.

As you move into future phases of the DEI Equity At Work™, every leader should have some degree of ownership of this work. This can happen once you are at a point when you are operationalizing DEI into your business. At this stage, it will be part of your regular operations, so all leaders can oversee DEI in their department or team and report on progress.

ESTABLISH DEI GOVERNANCE

This step can be implemented in many different ways. Governance, in short, is how you will organize your work, provide oversight, and insert checks and balances. It provides an important framework not only for what work will be done, but also for who will be involved and what the accountabilities look like. Some of my company's clients are very loose with this, while others live and die by governance. If you are a public company, governance will be a bigger deal all around, and you will likely have standards to follow for oversight and reporting as part of that.

As a general rule, governance typically includes:

- Purpose statement
- Guiding principles and bylaws
- Mission and scope of work
- Leadership structure specific to DEI work and key responsibilities
- Supporting roles, term timeframes per role, expectations, appointment process
- Integration with other teams
- Meeting structure and cadence
- Note-taking and communication expectations
- Decision-making guidelines
- Issue tracking and resolution processes
- Oversight and checks and balances
- Budget and approval process

- Results measurement process, frequency, and metrics
- Change management process and change communications framework

All of the governance topics outlined above need to be thoughtfully considered. Where I typically see variances is in how formalized the governance is. The degree of formality should align with your organization's culture and norms. If your company tends to manage more fluidly, thinking of governance as a set of guidelines and guardrails likely makes the most sense. At the same time, more formal, public, and highly regulated organizations will need a much more rigid structure. Regardless of how formal your process is, remember that good governance gets things done!

CONDUCT DEI SESSIONS FOR LEADERS

A common mistake organizations make is jumping straight to training their entire organization, often grouping employees who work at varying levels of seniority. While this may be the most efficient way to roll out training, it is not the most effective. Your most senior leaders must be the first to go through any DEI education so they can all be using the same language and be prepared for questions and challenges that will inevitably bubble up from the rest of the organization as it goes through DEI training. The best practice here is to structure the rollout of your DEI education as a cascade down and across the organization, from senior leaders down to middle management and then down to the balance of employees. This initial training for senior leaders, and then for all leaders, is best done as a workshop-style session or series of sessions where participants can ask questions freely among their peers, identify potential roadblocks and challenges, and discuss how to respond to various questions that will arise.

These early sessions can also be terrific opportunities for leaders to brainstorm how they want DEI to be experienced at your organization and what role each of them plays in making that happen. This can and should extend beyond training into the day-to-day ways everyone works together, both internally and externally, in the organization. For teams at step one of their DEI journey, we typically do education for the senior leadership team to help them identify DEI opportunities and set DEI goals. Once those are identified, you can incorporate them into your training as you begin to cascade it down and across your organization.

DEI training is most effective when done as an inter-active discussion, ideally in person. Many of the concepts sound simple—after all, few of us start our days thinking about how to exclude rather than include others—so it can take some discussion to tease out what about these ideas is hard or what is keeping them from happening naturally today. This also helps employees internalize the principles of DEI and feel more invested in being part of the solution or path forward.

BEGIN ACTIVITIES TO RAISE AWARENESS ABOUT DEI

This is a great place to have fun with your DEI work. It can include cultural observances, education about various DEI holidays and notable figures, celebrations of DEI wins at your organization, information about outreach in your community that relates to your mission with DEI, and so much more. Anything that highlights DEI in action is great here because you will start to get it in the day-to-day language of your employees, and this will generate even more ideas of what you can include in your DEI plans.

Here is an example of an educational flyer we created for a client to align with a monthly DEI celebration:

This is also a great time to think about driving engagement. Some of our clients have internally competitive cultures (in a healthy way!), and hold contests that test employees' knowledge about a topic they posted information on and awarding prizes to the winners. Others maintain ongoing digital suggestion boxes, post the submitted ideas, and celebrate the employees who contribute them. You can bring a lot of fun and creativity to this exercise, and the more you do, the more the concepts will stick with your employees.

Now that we've covered the essential steps for "Setting the DEI Foundation," let's go over the key cultural dependencies you need to have in place at this stage for your investment in DEI to work.

PSYCHOLOGICALLY SAFE WORK ENVIRONMENT

This needs to underpin all of your DEI work because you cannot have inclusion without psychological safety. Psychological safety is a term coined by researcher Amy Edmondson[9] that describes a work environment where employees can speak up and show up as their full, authentic selves without fear of retribution or exclusion. Her research shows that psychologically safe teams outperform those that are not in productivity, risk mitigation, safety, engagement, and innovation. Why? Because employees feel safe asking questions, speaking up, and/or challenging the status quo, and which often leads to better solutions.

---

[9] https://amycedmondson.com/psychological-safety/

Psychological safety can be a core tenet for an organization, but it is experienced at a situational level because that is where employees directly interact with each other. An employee may feel psychologically safe in one group and not another, largely dictated by the style of each group's leader. If that leader defers to leadership without question, expects employees to "fall in line" with corporate direction without providing space for discussion, or shames employees who speak up, challenge, or ask questions, that leader is not creating a psychologically safe environment.

Psychological safety is critical to DEI because it prioritizes creating work environments where everyone feels seen, heard, and valued for who they are. This, in turn, builds trust and creates opportunities for employees of many different experiences, demographics, and perspectives to contribute and be part of something bigger than themselves. It also inherently relies on equity to ensure everyone has an opportunity to contribute. Contributions need to be made in a respectful manner that fits the culture of the organization. As long as psychological safety is a consistent focus across leaders, they can create an environment where ideas flow freely.

In a psychologically safe work environment, trust and respect are cornerstones of the culture; mistakes are viewed as opportunities to learn, not failures; a "we" orientation—as opposed to a "me" orientation—prevails; candor and honesty are the norm. Employees feel their team members and boss have their back, that they will be valued for doing the right thing, and that they and others are treated fairly.

Here is a checklist to follow to make sure you are doing your part to create a psychologically safe environment at work:

Psychological Safety Comes From Small, Day-to-Day Actions

☑ Clear, consistent expectations are set up front

☑ Integrity and honesty are core values

☑ Leaders and peers actively listen

☑ The "why" is always clear

☑ It is ok to say "I don't know" or "I don't understand."

☑ It is ok to say, "I have another idea."

☑ Positive, inclusive behavior is recognized and rewarded

☑ Mistakes are viewed as learning opportunities

☑ Everyone feels like they are "in it" together

I have had clients insist their environment was psychologically safe when it was not, and it caused major setbacks in our DEI work and for the organization overall. If you communicate to your organization that everyone can be their full, authentic self at work and then punish people for doing so, your employees will turn on you quickly. You will have a big drop in trust and engagement, and employees will leave. DEI will be blamed when what you have really done is put DEI on top of a broken foundation.

I recommend you survey your organization to gauge how psychologically safe they feel, using the indicators in the checklist above. Perception is everything with this. If they don't feel safe, that feeling is valid and needs to be addressed before you invest any more time or budget in your DEI work.

Here is a sample survey that my team and I use with clients to gather their perceptions of the elements of psychological safety. This helps us determine where we need to start on culture work and how to structure DEI education and early work steps.

Leader Culture Survey

Thank you so much for taking this survey. The results will help us understand the current state of the culture at [INSERT COMPANY NAME]

All responses will be kept strictly confidential and will only be shared in aggregate. You will not be asked to share your name or any identifying information

* Indicates required question

What does success at [INSERT COMPANY NAME] look like to you? *

I look forward to coming to work *

	1	2	3	4	5	
Strongly Disagree	○	○	○	○	○	Strongly Agree

I feel like the majority of our team look forward to coming to work *

	1	2	3	4	5	
Strongly Disagree	○	○	○	○	○	Strongly Agree

I feel like we have a positive culture *

	1	2	3	4	5	
Strongly Disagree	○	○	○	○	○	Strongly Agree

I feel like our culture is people-first *

	1	2	3	4	5	
Strongly Disagree	○	○	○	○	○	Strongly Agree

I feel like I can be my full self at work *

	1	2	3	4	5	
Strongly Disagree	○	○	○	○	○	Strongly Agree

I am clear about the goals we are working toward as a team *

	1	2	3	4	5	
Strongly Disagree	○	○	○	○	○	Strongly Agree

I feel clear about my personal goals and how they fit into the bigger team goals *

	1	2	3	4	5	
Strongly Disagree	○	○	○	○	○	Strongly Agree

I feel like we collaborate well to solve problems *

	1	2	3	4	5	
Strongly Disagree	○	○	○	○	○	Strongly Agree

I feel like we have clear communication *

	1	2	3	4	5	
Strongly Disagree	○	○	○	○	○	Strongly Agree

I feel like it is easy to speak up about what is on my mind *

	1	2	3	4	5	
Strongly Disagree	○	○	○	○	○	Strongly Agree

I feel like continuous learning is valued here *

	1	2	3	4	5	
Strongly Disagree	○	○	○	○	○	Strongly Agree

I feel like we can try new approaches even if we don't know if the outcome will work *

	1	2	3	4	5	
Strongly Disagree	○	○	○	○	○	Strongly Agree

I feel like it is ok to try something new and fail *

	1	2	3	4	5	
Strongly Disagree	○	○	○	○	○	Strongly Agree

If I make a mistake, I don't feel like it is held against me *

	1	2	3	4	5	
Strongly Disagree	○	○	○	○	○	Strongly Agree

I feel like how we treat others is valued more than how we perform *

	1	2	3	4	5	
Strongly Disagree	○	○	○	○	○	Strongly Agree

I feel like how we treat others is valued equally to how we perform *

	1	2	3	4	5	
Strongly Disagree	○	○	○	○	○	Strongly Agree

I feel like we can talk about tough issues here *

	1	2	3	4	5	
Strongly Disagree	○	○	○	○	○	Strongly Agree

I feel like we are able to have healthy dialogue when there is a disagreement *

	1	2	3	4	5	
Strongly Disagree	○	○	○	○	○	Strongly Agree

I feel like our leadership team regularly checks in with team members about how *
they are doing personally

	1	2	3	4	5	
Strongly Disagree	○	○	○	○	○	Strongly Agree

I feel safe sharing my opinion even if it doesn't align with other leaders *

	1	2	3	4	5	
Strongly Disagree	○	○	○	○	○	Strongly Agree

No one on this team would intentionally undermine me or try to make me look *
bad in front of others

	1	2	3	4	5	
Strongly Disagree	○	○	○	○	○	Strongly Agree

I feel like we are one team, (whether someone works for [INSERT COMPANY *
NAME] or [INSERT COMPANY NAME])

	1	2	3	4	5	
Strongly Disagree	○	○	○	○	○	Strongly Agree

[OPTIONAL] Is there anything else you'd like to share?

Your answer

Submit

Scan the QR code to access a digital version
of the Leader Culture survey:

Password: DoDEIRight

You can use this survey to establish a baseline and then, as you implement changes, conduct it again to gauge whether your changes are having the desired impact. As you gather feedback, you can also slice the data in various ways, such as by level, tenure, and function, to understand any variances across the organization.

This outlines the progression we recommend to clients when peeling back the onion on psychological safety:

Psychological Safety Progression – Process & Structure

FOUNDATIONAL

- Norms and values that include integrity, honesty, active listening, and the importance of teamwork are established, communicated, and consistently adhered to

- DEI training is complete for all employees and is part of onboarding for all new employees

- Zero tolerance for bad behavior is consistently adhered to

- The "why" is part of all communication

- Doing the right thing is celebrated and reinforced consistently

- Multiple forums led by various levels of leaders are established for gathering feedback (roundtables, 1:1s, office hours, etc.), with feedback loops to share outcomes

- All leaders are coached on how to provide feedback

- Accessibility is provided to support all employee needs to meet people where they are

ADVANCED

Psychological Safety Progression – Organizational Feedback

The Question We Want to Answer	How We Answer The Question	What The Answer Tells Us
1 | How psychologically safe is the organization feeling in total?	Monthly pulse survey asking: • Do you enjoy working here? • Do you feel that doing the right thing is valued? • Do you feel you can speak up if you have an idea? • Do you feel safe speaking up if you have made a mistake?	The overall feeling of psychological safety for the organization
2 | Does this align with the feedback from employee relations (ER)?	• Review ER calls monthly • Identify themes related to psych safety and what % of employees raised each theme	If employees are contacting ER with psych safety issues, and if ER calls align with employee sentiment
3 | Are there any differences between leaders and staff?	• Keep total org results • Parse data into leaders vs staff • Compare responses	Variances by level
4 | Are there differences based on tenure?	• Continue above and add parsing based on tenure	Variances by tenure
5 | How do different roles compare?	• Continue above and add parsing based on role	Variances by role
6 | How do different demographic groups compare?	• Continue above and add parsing based on demographics	Variances by demographic

PEOPLE-FOCUSED COMPANY MISSION, VALUES, AND KPIS

DEI is about putting people first, and if you do not have a focus on people as part of your culture, DEI will not work. If you are in an organization whose mission and values are entirely focused on clients, customer service, and communities but lack any mention of what it aims to provide its employees, now is the time to revisit that. I am not talking about being people-focused instead of business-focused or service-focused; instead, these all need to go hand-in-hand.

The mission captures your organization's purpose. My company, Equity At Work™'s, for example, aims to create workplaces where everyone can thrive through customized DEI solutions that deliver high-impact results.

The values are the core tenets that you operate under and typically represent behaviors you want to see across your employees. They are the qualities that define your organization. Equity At Work™'s values are: focused on purpose and impact; innovative; gritty and resourceful; highest integrity with a commitment to excel; and team and partnership builders.

Finally, the Key Performance Indicators (KPIs) are the ways you measure your performance. People-oriented KPIs include engagement scores, internal Net Promoter Scores (NPS) that measure how likely an employee is to recommend working at the company to a friend or family member, tenure, voluntary turnover, and personal impact. These should go with other business KPIs such as sales, margin, and net income, as well as customer or client satisfaction rates, repeat customers or clients, and how likely they would be to refer others to you. Equity At Work™'s KPIs include a mix of all of the above.

Integrating a people focus into all these elements ensures that you keep your employee value proposition stays top of mind as you make business decisions. If your goal is to have DEI become part of your organization's DNA, you will need to have this people focus solidly in place.

BEHAVIOR MEASURED AND WEIGHED EQUALLY OR MORE HEAVILY THAN PERFORMANCE

Have you ever worked in an organization where a top performer got away with bad behavior because they were deemed a superstar? That is an environment where, regardless of the lip service given, only results matter, not how someone achieved those results. Measuring behavior goes hand-in-hand with psychological safety because you need how employees treat each other to be valued to have a psychologically safe environment. This is especially important for people in senior-level roles because they set an example for others. It is also imperative for DEI to work because DEI is all about how you treat your people.

How do you measure behavior? Regular organization-wide engagement surveys will help you gauge behavior overall. Ideally, you will collect enough data from respondents—while keeping the necessary elements private so they are confidential—so that you can see if there are variances by demographic, level, function, location, etc. Regular pulse checks can then supplement this with a handful of questions about behavior and psychological safety. You can also incorporate behavioral expectations into job descriptions and performance reviews, and get input from the key people who work with each individual about how well they are meeting these expectations. Finally, you will need to have a mechanism for employees to report negative behavior, especially biased, discriminatory, or harassing behavior, to human resources and/or employee relations, so any need for intervention and action can be determined and implemented. These incidents should also be tracked and incorporated into overall reporting about the behavioral health of the organization.

The final element here is making sure your employees are viewed and referenced as people, not resources. I worked with one client where the CEO kept referring to her people in the field organization as labor costs. This spoke volumes to me and to her senior leadership team, who had to talk in her language to connect with her. That is a slippery slope because it is just a matter of time before that term goes past the leadership team and out into the broader organization. That will make employees feel completely undervalued and that leaders are out of touch with their daily work experience. The first recommendation I had for that senior leadership team was to get out in the field and spend days pitching in and working side by side with their employees. The CEO needed to remember she had people in the field who were totally reliant on her and her team to do right by them.

KEY TAKEAWAYS

- Setting the DEI Foundation includes compliance work, defining what diversity, equity, and inclusion mean to your organization, gathering input, setting goals, defining champions and owners, establishing governance, providing education for senior leaders, and beginning to raise awareness about DEI across your organization.

- Input needs to come from every part of the organization.

- Champions and Owners need to be ready to walk the walk, not just talk the talk.

- Governance should be established in line with your company's culture.

- Leaders need to go through training before the rest of the organization so they can develop a common understanding and language for DEI, get aligned as a leadership team on the vision for the organization, and be ready to answer questions and manage tough conversations.

- Do not move forward with your DEI plans unless you have strong psychological safety, measurements in place for behavioral expectations, a people-focused mission, values, and KPIs, and value behavior equally or more than results.

CHAPTER 5

OPERATIONALIZING DEI

More times than I can count, I have met leaders who tell me their organization has identified goals and a strategy for their DEI work, and sometimes even a roadmap, but they do not know what to do next. They are stuck moving from idea to execution, even when their leaders are aligned. Typically, this is because the next steps of implementing the strategy will thrust them into tackling a number of things without clarity on what should come first. This work may also lead to tough conversations that they are nervous about, as sensitive areas are addressed.

Once you cover the foundational elements of DEI work, it is time to make DEI part of your organization's DNA. The steps that are part of operationalizing DEI focus on integrating DEI into all the ways your organization functions. This includes process, program, policy, and benefit updates, as well as tracking progress and establishing accountability so there is a consistent focus on and ownership of the work. This is where the proverbial rubber meets the road. Let's dive in.

Operationalizing DEI

Analyze workforce data and
benchmarks; update roadmap

Define metrics and sources for KPI
measurement, launch dashboard

Establish senior leader accountability
for achieving DEI goals

Conduct DEI education sessions for all
employees to build awareness and
skills

Create DEI internal and external
communication & feedback plans

**Essential DEI
Steps**

Update employee policies and benefits
to be fully inclusive

Update outreach, recruiting, hiring,
compensation, development, review,
promotion, and succession planning to
remove bias and be fully equitable

Establish ERGs & affinity groups

Celebrate DEI wins

Collaboration, Communication,
Learning & Feedback Highly Valued

**Culture
Requirements**

Team Norms Well Defined and
Followed

ANALYZE WORKFORCE DATA AND BENCHMARKS; UPDATE ROADMAP

This stage starts with taking an honest look at where you are today using data. This data includes your own internal HR data as well as industry and competitor data, where it is available, for benchmarks and points of comparison.

At a high level, here is how we at Equity At Work™ think about the story organizational data tells us related to DEI:

This graphic can help you identify ways to align metrics and KPIs with your internal and external DEI work. You do not need to use all of these, especially if you are at the beginning of your DEI journey. You can select a handful of metrics that align with your biggest areas of focus and then layer in additional ones as you expand your scope and expertise.

Now that you have a sense of how data aligns with different aspects of DEI, it is time to dig into your employee data from HR. This data can tell you a ton about where you have opportunities, but it usually takes digging below total company-level data to spot them. What I love about using data is that it is black and white, and it helps people visualize a problem that could feel very conceptual or subjective to them if they have not had direct experience with bias in the workplace. When you look at employee data, you want to gather it at the employee level and remove any personal identifiers for privacy and security purposes.

The data you want to gather per employee is listed below:

Demographic Data Dimensions

- From employee HR data:
  - ○ Gender
  - ○ Race
  - ○ Age
- Opt-in through self-ID campaign, as available:
  - ○ LGBTQIA+
  - ○ Disability
  - ○ Veteran status
  - ○ Country of origin
  - ○ Ethnicity
  - ○ Native language

Demographic Data Attributes

- Total company
- Business unit
- Senior Leadership Team line of reporting
- Function
- Level
- Location
- Salaried vs hourly
- Full-time vs part-time, seasonal vs temp

Employee Lifecycle Data

- Tenure
  - Example breakouts: 0-6 mo., 6-12 mo., 1-3 yr, 3-5 yr, 5-10 yr, 10+ yr
  - Promotions
  - Turnover
  - Voluntary vs non + reason codes
- Hiring
  - Demographics + recruit-to-hire ratios
- Training/professional development
  - Number of hours
  - Mandatory vs optional
  - Leadership development participation
- Paid leave
  - Demographics of who takes leave, who returns, and tenure following leave

Current State Snapshot and Trends Over Time

- Determine time breaks
  - Year-over-year, quarter-over-quarter, or other, based on hiring, promotion, and acquisition cycles
- Align census data as applicable
- Align industry benchmark/trend data as applicable
- Align performance vs goals as applicable
- Set a baseline in order to track trends over time as you add more data

Once you've pulled and organized your data, you can dig into your analysis and make comparisons across different demographics and dimensions.

Here are a few examples of ways my team and I have looked at data:

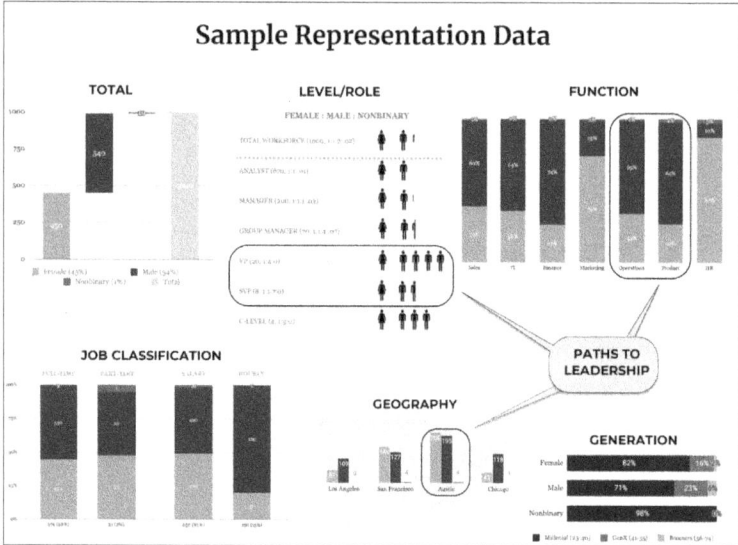

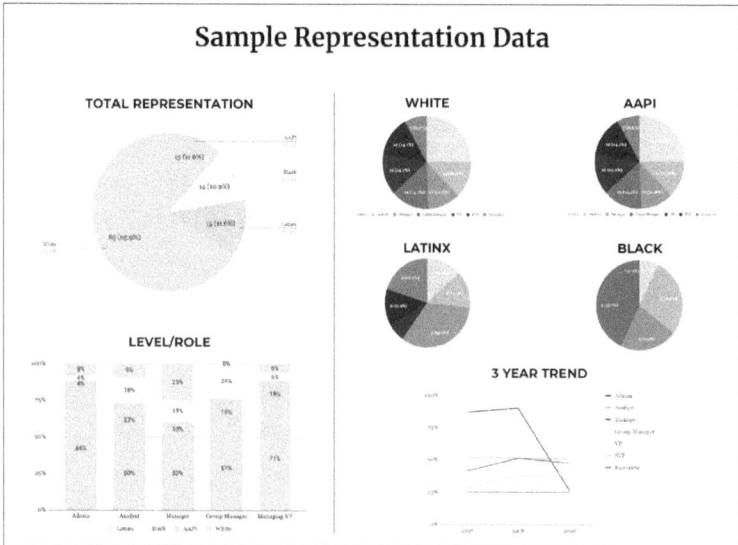

Sample Representation Data

Sample Promotion and Leave Data

Your total company data will give you an overall indication of how you are performing today and where broad DEI opportunities exist. The most valuable information, however, typically becomes clear when you slice the data to do comparisons across demographic dimensions and attributes. This is where you can spot variances across dimensions and see if they make sense or are indicators of bias creeping into processes or leader decisions.

Once you have set up your internal views, the next step is to look at external data. Industry data can provide you with context for how you are doing compared to the total workforce and to your industry specifically. Great data sources for the US market are the most recent Census data and the US Bureau of Labor Statistics (BLS)[10]. There are also consulting and research firms that do regular reviews of overall workplace and industry trends. These are easily found through online searches.

For example, here is a snapshot of the employable workforce in the US based on 2022 BLS data[11]:

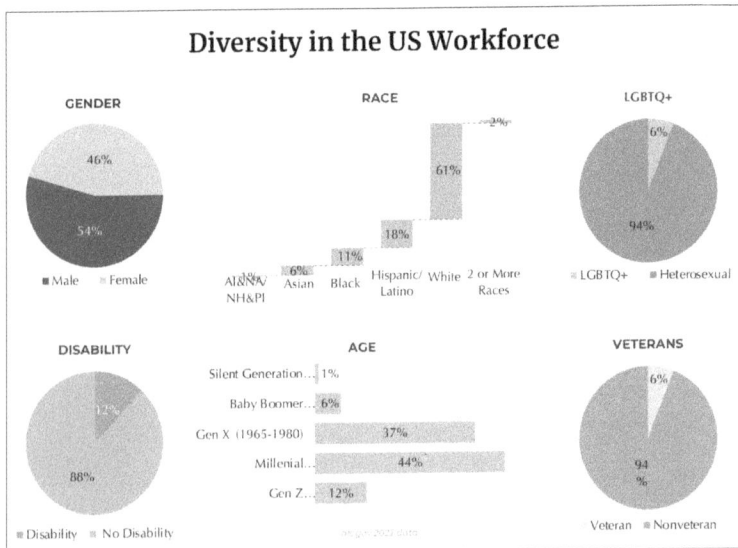

Diversity in the US Workforce

GENDER: Male 54%, Female 46%

RACE: AI&AN/NH&PI 1%, Asian 6%, Black 11%, Hispanic/Latino 18%, White 61%, 2 or More Races 2%

LGBTQ+: LGBTQ+ 6%, Heterosexual 94%

DISABILITY: Disability 12%, No Disability 88%

AGE: Silent Generation... 1%, Baby Boomer... 6%, Gen X (1965-1980) 37%, Millenial... 44%, Gen Z... 12%

VETERANS: Veteran 6%, Nonveteran 94%

---

[10] https://www.bls.gov/
[11] https://www.bls.gov/

When you use any of this data, remember that organizations with fewer than fifty employees are not required to report their data, and that many employees who are LGBTQIA+, disabled, and/or veterans do not choose to share this information with their employers as it is not mandated. When I look at the LGBTQIA+ numbers in this graph, I assume that the real number is at least twice what is shown here. I feel confident about that because I also review findings from organizations that focus on supporting LGBTQIA+ employees in the workplace that do their own surveys. That does not give me a precise number, but I do get a directional sense of how large this population is in the workplace, which is still a good point of reference. This is a place where you do not want perfection to be the enemy of the good. Use what you can pull and put the necessary caveats around it.

Census data can also provide a very broad overview of diversity specific to race and gender. For example, here is one graphic that the US Census Bureau has created to show the density of racial diversity by state[12]. This can be helpful if you want to see this dynamic for multiple locations you operate in:

---

[12]   https://www.census.gov/library/visualizations/2021/dec/racial-and-ethnic-diversity-index.html

Racial and Ethnic Diversity Index by State: 2020

The Diversity Index tells us the chance that two people chosen at random will be from different racial and ethnic groups.

Diversity Index
- 65.0% or more
- 55.0 to 64.9%
- 45.0 to 54.9%
- 35.0 to 44.9%
- Less than 35.0%

AK 40.4%, WA 58.9%, OR 46.5%, CA 69.0%, NV 68.8%, UT 40.3%, AZ 61.3%, ID 35.9%, MT 30.1%, WY 32.4%, CO 52.7%, NM 63.0%, ND 32.6%, SD 35.8%, NE 40.8%, KS 48.4%, OK 59.5%, TX 67.0%, MN 40.5%, IA 30.8%, MO 40.9%, AR 49.0%, LA 58.6%, WI 37.0%, IL 67.5%, MI 49.2%, IN 40.3%, KY 32.8%, TN 46.8%, MS 55.0%, AL 52.1%, OH 40.4%, WV 20.2%, GA 64.7%, FL 64.1%, SC 54.0%, NC 57.0%, VA 61.8%, PA 44.0%, NY 65.8%, VT 20.2%, ME 18.5%, NH 23.6%, MA 51.6%, RI 48.6%, CT 55.7%, NJ 65.8%, DE 59.6%, MD 67.3%, DC 67.2%, HI 76.0%, PR 2.2%

United States®
Census
Bureau

U.S. Department of Commerce
U.S. CENSUS BUREAU
census.gov

Source: 2020 Census Redistricting Data
(Public Law 94-171) Summary File

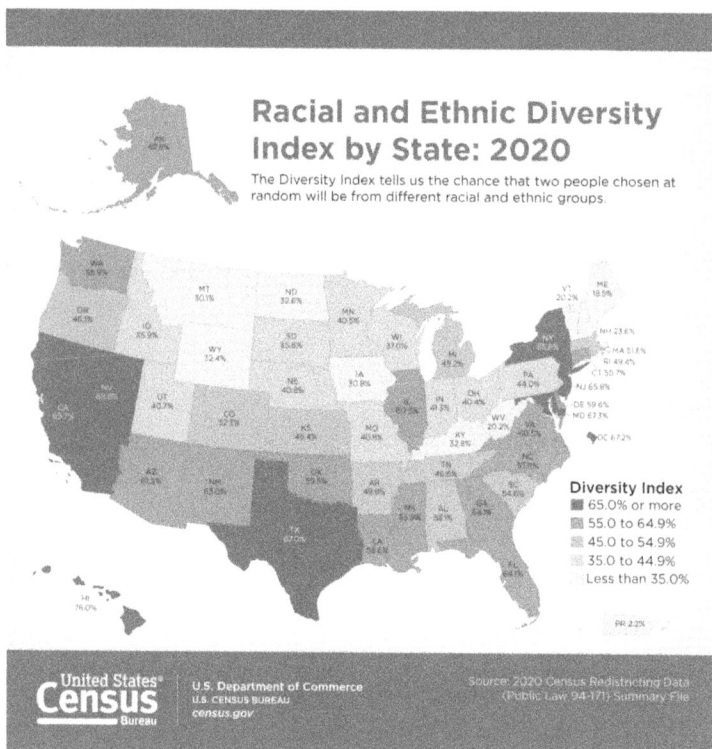

Many clients ask if they should aim to match the diversity of the state, county, or city in which they operate. I think it is helpful to be aware of the diversity in these areas, coupled with the diversity within your industry and the schools you are recruiting from. Together, those data points can help you set realistic goals for the makeup of your workforce. However, you do not want to have a hard-set rule to match your community's makeup exactly, as that can be interpreted as a quota.

After completing your analysis, it can be helpful to summarize your findings from both the data work and the feedback you gathered in your setting the foundation work so that it is all in one place.

Here is an example SWOT analysis that pulls all those pieces into one summary graphic:

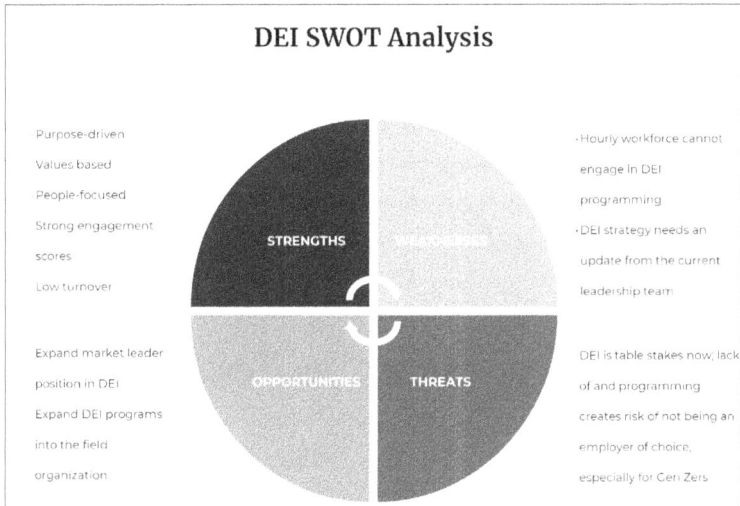

DEI SWOT Analysis

STRENGTHS
Purpose-driven
Values based
People-focused
Strong engagement
scores
Low turnover

WEAKNESSES
· Hourly workforce cannot
engage in DEI
programming
· DEI strategy needs an
update from the current
leadership team

OPPORTUNITIES
Expand market leader
position in DEI
Expand DEI programs
into the field
organization

THREATS
DEI is table stakes now; lack
of and programming
creates risk of not being an
employer of choice,
especially for Gen Zers

DEFINE SOURCES AND METRICS FOR KPI MEASUREMENT, LAUNCH DEI DASHBOARD

Once you have reviewed all the industry and competitor data and determined what is most relevant to you, you can identify the best sources for that information and determine how frequently it will be updated. You want your sources to do two things for you: provide sound insights and be able to withstand challenge. Therefore, it is important to select sources that are reliable, have a meaningful sample size, and employ sound methodology for gathering and analyzing their findings. You also want to narrow down your list to a handful because it is easy to fall into analysis paralysis here. Focus on the ones that give you good direction on where you need to go and are most relatable to your business and culture, and you will be in good shape.

After you have completed your internal data review in the previous step, you will have a good idea of which aspects you want to continuously track as indicators of whether your DEI work is having an impact. Beyond the overall makeup of the organization over time, typically a combination of promotion data (time to promotion by demographic, how that varies across locations, departments and levels, and the diversity of each promotion group) and turnover data (voluntary versus involuntary by demographic, and how that varies across locations, departments, levels and tenure) are included here. Compensation can also be a big one to look at, especially if you are in a volatile industry or doing a lot of acquisitions. Professional development and mentoring can be important if one of your challenges is getting certain employee demographics to be better represented at more senior levels.

Beyond your HR data, it is also good to include engagement and NPS scores. If there are questions in your engagement survey that are specific to DEI, you'll want to call those out separately from the overall score. Don't forget to include metrics that measure the impact you are having externally through supplier diversity programs (percent of total supplier/ vendor spend, money spent on diverse suppliers), community outreach (hours and/or money donated), and any other external activities. You can use your external sources to provide context and/or benchmarks for how you are doing compared to your industry and/or competitors.

Once you've finalized what you are going to measure, you will need to determine how often you want to update the data. Organizations generally bring in new employees once a year and promote once or twice a year usually refresh their data annually. Organizations that are more dynamic in their recruiting, promotions, and acquisitions and want to measure the impact of specific initiatives more quickly will typically refresh more often.

The final step here is to build out a dashboard that captures your key measurements. I recommend you create a few versions of these dashboards, one more detailed for leaders to use in decision-making and a higher-level one to provide transparency to the organization on your DEI goals and progress. If you are a public company, you will also want to use the elements of the dashboard (and possibly the dashboard itself) in your annual ESG reporting. It is important to create communication to accompany dashboards that explain how to read them and what the key takeaways are.

There is no one right way to create a DEI dashboard. Best practice is to have it be one of many tools in your communication toolbelt, meaning it uses the same branding and language that you use in your other communications. My team and I have built dashboards that feel very corporate, others that are more playful, and some in between. Coming up with a format that employees are excited to review is worth spending time on.

Here are a few examples that we have built for clients:

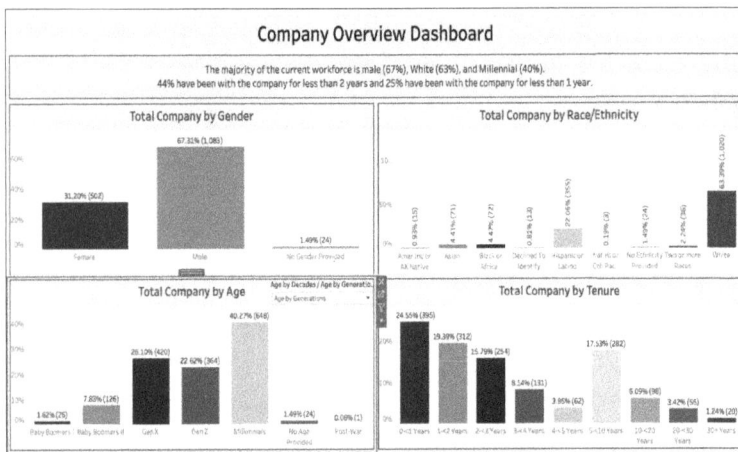

Much like my recommended approach with training, dashboards are best rolled out in a cascade approach from the most senior leaders down through the organization. Remember, you will want to provide talking points that explain how to read it and what the key takeaways are. Take the time to ensure each level of your organization understands the dashboard before you go to the next level, both in terms of its purpose and its content. It is also important to be prepared with answers to any anticipated questions, especially about how employees can help improve any of the metrics you have identified as opportunities. This is a great way to bring the organization together around a common goal.

ESTABLISH SENIOR-LEVEL ACCOUNTABILITY FOR ACHIEVING DEI GOALS

This is a critical step. Without accountability, no one will be fully responsible for your DEI goals being accomplished. The CEO needs to be the ultimate owner of DEI and a visible, vocal leader on it, but the specific areas of work on your roadmap each need their own senior leader who is accountable. Early in an organization's DEI journey, it is typical for only a few members of the senior leadership team to be accountable for aspects of DEI since it typically involves research, analysis, and testing of a few programs or new training. However, as the organization evolves to have more robust plans and roadmaps, every senior leader needs to have DEI goals they are accountable for delivering.

For context, companies' integration of Environmental, Social, and Governance (ESG) metrics into compensation plans is now over seventy-five percent. When looking at the Russell 3000, over eighty percent of companies with revenues of $50 billion and higher do the same[13]. These organizations tie ESG performance to compensation for the full C-suite and, in many cases, one to two levels below.

---

[13] https://www.conference-board.org/publications/ESG-performance-metrics-in-executive-compensation-plans

At the most senior level, an executive who is accountable for an aspect of DEI work will most likely delegate tasks to members of his, her, or their team. This is typically the most effective way to accomplish the work, and it has the added benefit of creating opportunities for many employees to play an important role in moving DEI forward. That being said, at the end of the day that executive is the one who will be held accountable for the work getting done and the goals being met.

When thinking through accountability, there are four aspects to consider:

1. Who the owner is, specifically who is in charge of directing the work, even if this is not who will do the work

2. What specific aspects of DEI they are responsible for, which can be solving a specific issue, launching a program, or something else

3. What goals, both quantitative and qualitative, they are responsible for achieving

4. How ownership will be measured in their performance review, including the impact on their raise and bonus

Here is an example to help illustrate how this works. Let's say you are working in a large retail organization. Your executive team has developed its DEI roadmap and identified priorities and goals for next year, and these have been divided up across the leadership team. Here is what one member of the team is accountable for:

1. Owner: SVP of Stores

2. Responsible for recruiting and retaining diverse talent in the field organization to better reflect and represent the needs of our customers

3. Goals for the year include:

- Improving outreach to potential field organization employees
- Removing bias from job descriptions and interviewing
- Improving retention in the field organization by 5 percentage points
- Improving engagement scores in the field organization overall by 5 percentage points and for historically underrepresented minority employees in the field by ten percentage points

4. These goals will comprise fifteen percent of their performance review rating, which directly impacts their raise. These goals also comprise 5 percent of their bonus calculation, which is lower than the performance review percentage because the majority of the bonus is calculated on the company meeting its financial goals.

Notice that the measurable metrics in the goals are for retention and engagement, while representation is more generalized. This is to help ensure that the SVP of Stores is not incentivized to meet a quota, whether specific or implied.

In the example above, the SVP of Stores has goals that they will need to partner with others in the organization, such as talent acquisition and employee engagement, to achieve. The reason the SVP of Stores is accountable for these goals is that they directly impact their business unit. The Chief Human Resources Officer may have similar accountabilities to what is outlined above for the SVP Stores, but they would span the entire organization. Having multiple leaders with the same goals can work if they are measured equally on them. If the weighting for one leader is much higher or lower than for the other, you can run into problems prioritizing their execution.

One word of caution here… as leaders delegate tasks down to their respective teams, there is always a risk of duplicative work springing up. This is where governance can be a huge help. Having someone on point to create visibility across teams into their tasks, timing, and participants can help eliminate duplicative efforts and make sure everyone is working together as efficiently and effectively as possible.

CONDUCT DEI EDUCATION SESSIONS FOR ALL EMPLOYEES TO BUILD AWARENESS AND SKILLS

Remember: The best practice here is to structure the rollout of your DEI education as a cascade down and across the organization, from senior leaders down to middle management and then down to the balance of employees. After you have completed training for all leaders as part of Setting the Foundation for DEI, you are now ready to roll out training to all of your employees.

Because this is DEI training, it is important to make it as inclusive as possible and to create safe spaces so employees can ask questions freely. In most cases, this means you will need to organize training into groups of peers so that no one feels they cannot speak up because their supervisor is in the room. That being said, it is great to have a senior leader who is a sponsor of DEI work participate to send a message about how important this training is. If this feels like it will stifle discussion, have the senior leader come in to kick off and set the tone and then step out for the remainder of the session.

These sessions are best done in smaller groups, in an interactive style that fosters a lot of discussion and allows for questions. Weaving in videos, breakout groups, scenarios, practice time, brainstorming partners, games, and other interactive activities caters to multiple learning styles and helps ensure the session is engaging.

I hear a lot of horror stories about DEI training gone wrong, from the use of racism scales to being lectured about white fragility. My number one rule with DEI training is to make it as accessible as possible, with no shaming or blaming. I want people to come away with their minds a little more open to a topic they may not have spent a lot of time thinking about before. And I want them to come away with at least one new thing to try after the session. I focus on practical, actionable topics that are directly relatable to their workplace experience.

Many topics can be included in DEI training. I always recommend starting with the definition of DEI and how it shows up at work so everyone is speaking the same language. Here are the most common topics my team and I cover in our workshops with clients:

#	TOPIC
	SETTING THE DEI FOUNDATION
	These topics provide all employees with a baseline knowledge of DEI and how it shows up in the workplace
1	DEI definitions and how they show up at work
2	Equity vs equality
3	Dimensions of diversity and how we each relate to them
4	Intersectionality
5	Unconscious bias and microaggressions

PUTTING DEI INTO ACTION	
These topics provide all employees with ways to put DEI into action at work	
6	Active listening and communication
7	Inclusive language
8	Practicing inclusion
9	Engaging across diverse teams
10	Empathy vs sympathy
11	Empathy in action
12	Being an upstander rather than a bystander
13	Allyship, advocacy, coaching, and mentoring
LEADER TOPICS	
These topics provide leaders with the skills and knowledge to incorporate the principles of DEI into how they work with and lead their teams	
14	Inclusive leadership
15	Psychological safety
16	Incorporating DEI into team norms
17	Unconscious bias 2.0: stripping bias out of decision-making
18	Constructive feedback (centered on DEI principles)
19	Navigating difficult conversations
20	Healthy conflict (centered on DEI principles)

SPECIALIZED TOPICS

These topics go deeper into specific areas of DEI
that typically apply to smaller audiences such as ERGs and HCI

21	Creating a mental-health-focused work environment
22	Building your business case for DEI
23	Extending DEI to your community
24	Content on DEI holidays, observances, and specific dimensions
25	Identifying and addressing burnout for yourself and your team (related to DEI)

This is not an exhaustive list of topics, but it should give you a good jumping-off point. Many of these can be bundled together, and it is always a good idea to reinforce earlier topics as you cover more advanced ones. Most importantly, all of these need to be put in the language of your culture at your organization and should directly address how this content helps your organization live out its promise to its employees and achieve its goals. The more you can tie the content to your values, mission, and key initiatives, the more impactful it will be.

CREATE DEI INTERNAL AND EXTERNAL COMMUNICATION PLANS AND FEEDBACK PLANS

Communication is essential not only to share information; when done well, it helps create trust, spurs ideas, and drives positive change. The number one rule with DEI communication is to create space to LISTEN. Respond promptly so employees know you heard them. People often think of organizational communication as what information you share with employees, investors, the press, and the general public. But this is only half of the equation! Feedback loops are an essential part of communication, especially with DEI, because you need to create a dialogue so you know what is working and what your opportunities are. The larger the organization, the more important feedback loops become, so you can get a read on the pulse of the organization. Your employees have lots of ideas— listen to them!

When creating communication plans, there are a number of elements to consider:

- What are we communicating about?
- Why are we communicating about this? Why now?
- What is the purpose of the communication? How can we tie it to our mission, vision, values, and/or KPIs?
- How important or urgent is this information?
- Who will develop the communication? Who will send out the communication? Does anyone need to review or approve the communication before it is shared?
- Who needs to receive the communication? In what order?
- What are the key points that need to be included? Do supplemental materials need to be provided, e.g., FAQs, website links, handouts, etc.?
- What channels will we use to send out the communication?
- When and how frequently will we send out the communication?
- How will we gather feedback?
- How will we follow up on the communication and feedback?

Here is an example communications plan checklist:

Topics To Address	Questions to Answer	Complete?
What needs to be communicated about?	○ What is happening? ○ When it is happening? ○ Why is it happening?	☐
How urgent is this communication?	○ Critical? (emergency, urgent) ○ Priority? (time-sensitive) ○ Important? (crucial for operations) ○ Relevant? (valuable for doing job) ○ Engaging/Social? (helpful or fun)	☐
Does anyone outside of Evolve need to review or sign off on the communication?	○ Do senior leaders need to see it in advance? ○ Do others?	☐
Who will <u>develop</u> the communication?	○ Who will write the communication?	☐
Who will <u>deliver</u> the communication?	○ Who will distribute or present the communication?	☐
Who will the communication go to?	○ Who needs to receive the communication?	☐
How will the communication be delivered?	○ What format will the communication be delivered in? Think about presentations, team meetings, intranet, postings in building, etc.	☐
What are the key messages we need to include?	○ What are we doing? ○ Why are we doing this? ○ What action is required? ○ What are the timing and next steps?	☐
Timing	○ When does this need to go out? ○ In what order across channels? ○ Is it one time or will it need to be repeated? If repeated, when?	☐

These elements need to be thought through for both internal and external communications. Anything you communicate externally should also be shared internally, and particularly with DEI, any external statements of support need to align with the organization's culture and employee experience. Additionally, communication should not be a once-and-done exercise. Communicate clearly and often. Repeat what is most important, and then repeat it again. Better to overcommunicate than risk someone missing the communication.

DEI is often communicated best through stories. If you are announcing a new DEI initiative, it can be powerful to include a quote from an employee about why this program is meaningful to them or why they are excited about it. Videos and pictures are terrific here, too, because they can show the personal impact of this work and show what DEI looks like in action.

The best practice is to integrate your DEI communications into all your existing communications channels and methods. Internally, it can be included on your internal portal, in Slack or Teams channels, in your newsletter, in town halls, posted around your offices or facilities, and in weekly team meetings. One organization I work with added a "DEI Minute" to their monthly meetings, and we use that time to cover an upcoming DEI-related holiday or observance, its meaning, and a brief Q&A. DEI should also be included in your recruiting materials and talking points, onboarding, and all standard training. This is part of making it part of your DNA, bringing it into all the ways you interact with your employees. Including it externally means it is part of your company website, social media, press releases, and quarterly and annual reports, typically in the ESG or corporate social responsibility sections.

Internal feedback loops can include virtual or physical suggestion boxes, a dedicated email box, or contacting designated employees in DEI roles. Posting questions or suggestions along with responses promptly is a vital part of the feedback loop, and the internal communication channels above are all good options for that. Be sure to document the questions, suggestions, responses, and any related explanations or future follow-ups, and make those accessible to everyone.

UPDATE EMPLOYEE POLICIES AND BENEFITS TO BE FULLY INCLUSIVE

This is a critical step to ensure your DEI work is embedded in the foundational parts of the organization. A great starting point for this is to think about your purpose in doing your DEI work and your goals. What is the ideal output from your work? How do you want your employees to feel about the organization once your DEI goals have been achieved? You can take that information and use it to inform which policies and practices need to be updated to enable those results.

A great tool to help you identify what needs to be updated is an employee-lifecycle visual. This should capture all the key ways employees interface with the organization and how they will progress in their careers.

Here is the employee lifecycle component of the framework I shared earlier:

Think through each step in your employee lifecycle and determine what policies and practices align with them, and of those, which ones need to be updated to be more inclusive. For example, do you want to ensure there is a plan for outreach to schools that have high levels of diversity for recruiting? That language can go into your policy for attraction. You may want to create programs to mentor employees by matching them with leaders who come from different backgrounds. That language can go into your development step for mentoring.

An empathy map can help you think through all the constituents you need to consider when updating your policies and practices .

Here is an example empathy map template:

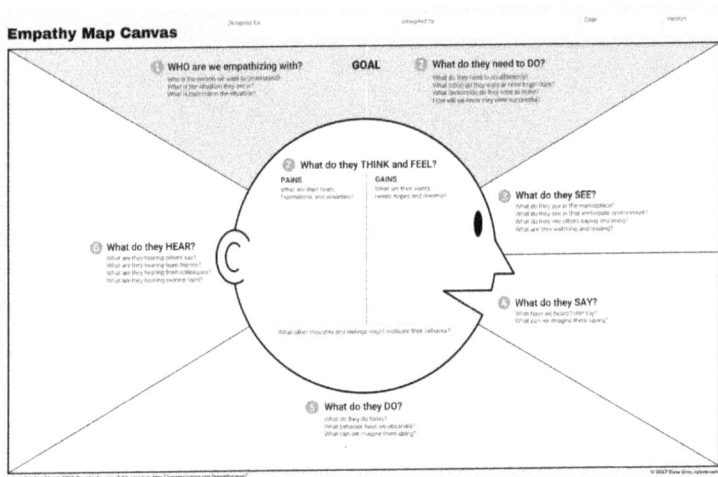

Empathy Map Canvas

You can create a generic company employee empathy map, but ideally, you will get more precise and create one for the different profiles or types of employees, drawing from your diversity demographics. Revisiting the Diversity Wheel can also be helpful here. You may decide you do not need to answer every question here and likely have others you want to think through. The main takeaway is to determine what different employees in your organization need and use that to inform how to update your policies and benefits.

The most common updates we have seen clients make recently are related to remote work, pronoun usage, parental leave, transgender employee support, flexible schedules, family planning, and family care. Remember, the language you use here is just as important as the content of the policies and practices. You want to communicate inclusion throughout.

UPDATE OUTREACH, RECRUITING, HIRING, COMPENSATION, DEVELOPMENT, REVIEW, PROMOTION, AND SUCCESSION PLANNING TO REMOVE BIAS AND BE FULLY EQUITABLE

This is where you bring policies and benefits into action, with a major focus on stripping out bias that could impact an employee's career opportunities. These processes will align with your employee lifecycle, and there may be others you want to include that are not listed. This is another great place to use your empathy maps so you can put yourself in the shoes of different employees going through these processes.

The analysis you did on your workforce will have identified where you have different outcomes for your employees based on their demographics and attributes. That gives you a great starting point for this step. Your DEI goals will help you determine how to prioritize this work. For example, if you are concerned that there is bias holding certain employees back from being promoted, you will want to start with reviews,

promotions, and succession planning. If you are more concerned initially with who you bring into your recruiting pipeline, you will want to prioritize outreach, recruiting, hiring,
and compensation. Development can include everything from
training to sponsorship, mentorship, and coaching, provided
internally and/or through external programs and resources.

Removing bias completely is impossible because we all
have biases that we are not fully aware of. Your goal here is
to ensure you are not embedding any bias into your processes,
thereby making the bias systemic. Having multiple people
involved in this work will help you identify those blind spots
and correct them. Another excellent method to use in rede-
signing these processes is to insert checks and balances so
that no one person is the decision-maker or gatekeeper of a
process. Having independent reviewers for hiring, review, and
promotion decisions can be a big help. Some organizations
have someone available to challenge points of view that could
be biased in those discussions, which has the added benefit of
creating learning opportunities.

A special note on compensation and pay equity: it is
important for organizations to establish a rigorous process
and a regular cadence for reviewing compensation to ensure
equal pay for equal work. If your organization or industry is
in a big growth mode, especially through acquisitions, you
will need to do this at least once a year. If you are in a slower-
paced organization or industry, every two to three years may
be fine. You will have to consider market dynamics, trends
with new employees coming out of school, and what your
competitors are doing. When you do a pay equity review, it
is critical that you look at base compensation, bonuses, and

benefits—the total package. Another critical element to consider is leveling. Quite often, I see organizations that have calibrated pay equally across levels, but historically underrepresented employees are not promoted at equal rates as those who are in the majority, even when their performance is equal. As a result, they do not have true pay equity. Leveling analysis needs to go hand in hand with compensation reviews. These will tie directly into your review, promotion, and succession planning processes.

As you make changes to your processes, be sure to track your progress after you have rolled out changes so you can see if they are delivering the desired impact. A lot of these processes need to be reviewed and refined on a regular basis to ensure the results are helping you reach your DEI goals. Remember, you are striving to make these processes as equitable as possible, so you are looking for consistent treatment while also ensuring support has been provided to enable your employees to operate on a level playing field.

ESTABLISH ERGS AND AFFINITY GROUPS

Employee Resource Groups (ERGs), sometimes called affinity groups or networks, are employee-led groups supported by the company, where employees who have a shared identity can gather and discuss aspects of this shared identity at work. ERGs can become hubs that generate terrific feedback, foster innovative problem-solving, and identify opportunities for greater employee support. They can also be catalysts for employees to build new relationships, find mentors, learn about other cultures, and collaborate on new ways to give back to the community.

ERGs typically provide opportunities for members to network, identify and brainstorm solutions for shared issues or concerns, engage in professional development, provide education to the broader organization on that identity, and identify ways to provide support and advocate if interested.

ERGs originated by including only members who identify with the ERG, and have evolved to also provide opportunities for allies, friends, and anyone who wants to learn more to engage. It is important to have some dedicated time for those who identify with the ERG so they have a safe space to discuss their needs. Dedicating additional time and opportunities for others to engage builds out a stronger support network and ensures no silos exist between ERG and non-ERG members. Looking at ways to provide information, education, and opportunities for celebration across the organization is a great way to leverage the power of the ERGs and get a company-wide benefit at the same time.

Some companies define areas that are in and out of scope for ERG consideration, based on their values, brand, and employee promise. For example, organizations often state that ERGs cannot be political in nature, as they could press agendas that are exclusionary for some employees. Some also will support interfaith groups but not religion-specific groups, so employees can come together to talk about how to support various faiths in the workplace, but not to say only one particular faith is supported.

An executive sponsor who is at a senior leadership level should join each ERG. This person can identify with the affinity group or be an ally to the group. The executive sponsor is there to demonstrate leadership support of the group and to provide a feedback loop to/from leadership on ideas and issues the ERG wants to raise to that level. What is most important is that this person is highly engaged and is willing to be a voice for the group in senior discussions. It is not a good idea to force a leader to be the sponsor of an ERG. You want their full buy-in so their participation feels authentic to the ERG members.

The ERG members should define the purpose and goals of that ERG and revisit them each year. These should be shared with the leadership team to ensure visibility into each ERG's mission. Additionally, having an opportunity for each ERG to share information about themselves in a regular company communication, such as a newsletter or town hall, is a great way to provide visibility.

ERG goals should be measurable to the greatest extent possible. Identifying metrics that are indicators of success is a great way to build momentum and ensure the ERG is staying focused on outcomes. Qualitative measures that look at sentiment are just as important as quantitative ones.

Light governance should also be applied within the ERG, including meeting cadence, a budget owner, an event planner, etc. For large ERGs, these roles can be distributed across a steering committee or ERG leader team and rotated every year or two.

Here is a simple graphic that summarizes the typical evolution of ERGs:

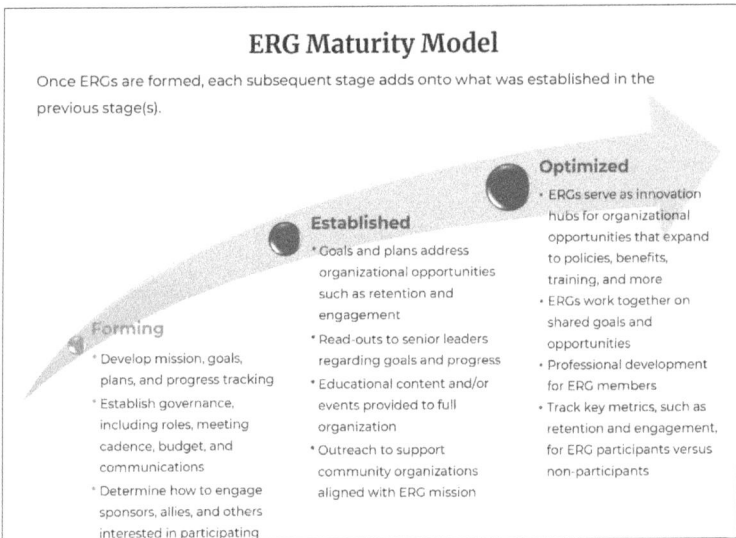

ERG Maturity Model

Once ERGs are formed, each subsequent stage adds onto what was established in the previous stage(s).

Forming
* Develop mission, goals, plans, and progress tracking
* Establish governance, including roles, meeting cadence, budget, and communications
* Determine how to engage sponsors, allies, and others interested in participating

Established
* Goals and plans address organizational opportunities such as retention and engagement
* Read-outs to senior leaders regarding goals and progress
* Educational content and/or events provided to full organization
* Outreach to support community organizations aligned with ERG mission

Optimized
* ERGs serve as innovation hubs for organizational opportunities that expand to policies, benefits, training, and more
* ERGs work together on shared goals and opportunities
* Professional development for ERG members
* Track key metrics, such as retention and engagement, for ERG participants versus non-participants

CELEBRATE DEI WINS

This is so important! It is so easy to get caught up in all the work that needs to be done that we forget to celebrate what has been accomplished. These celebrations go a long way in sustaining momentum and keeping the benefits of this work top of mind for everyone.

Whether big or small, a win is a win and deserves recognition. Leveraging all the elements of your communication plan will ensure the word gets out across the organization and externally. Celebrations can come in many forms: prizes, awards, recognition in key meetings, spotlights on your portal or in your newsletter, and more. Design your celebrations to align with your organization's culture and language, and be sure to highlight individual, team, and total company contributions.

Here are two examples of DEI celebrations, recognizing an individual's contribution and the other of a company's leadership in its industry. Both were shared company-wide and on social media.

Now that we've covered the essential steps for "Operationalizing DEI," let's review the key cultural dependencies you need to have in place at this stage for your investment in DEI to work.

COLLABORATION, COMMUNICATION, LEARNING, AND FEEDBACK ARE HIGHLY VALUED

This cultural requirement focuses on your employees' development. The collaboration component is to help people feel like they are part of something bigger than themselves and are connected to others, both foundational to inclusion. Collaboration can exist both within and across teams and should mitigate any unhealthy internal competition that may prioritize results over behavior.

The focus on communication helps employees stay connected and have visibility into the "why" of their work and the vision for the company. This also bolsters inclusion, and transparency goes a long way toward building trust and engagement. Transparency also helps everyone spot instances of bias and inequity and helps those get addressed much more quickly. Finally, open lines of communication establish flows of input to and from employees as cultural norms.

Remember, communication is as much about listening as it is about talking. Don't feel compelled to always jump to action or have an answer. Creating space to listen and reflecting back what you have heard to ensure you understood correctly are incredibly important parts of the equation. It is very likely tough conversations need to happen—tough to hear, tough to share, and maybe even tough to realize how something or someone in your company is contributing to the problem. You need to engage in these conversations so you can identify and get to the core of what may be causing issues for your people. This will create your company's compass for moving forward.

Curiosity and inquisitiveness are welcomed and held in high regard in this kind of culture, creating tremendous opportunities for learning on the job rather than having to wait for formal training. This also creates opportunities for ongoing feedback in a more fluid coaching style, as opposed to holding any feedback until a formal review at the end of the year. This does not mean employees are nitpicked constantly. Instead, they are recognized for doing well, coached when they need to do something differently, and provided resources when they need extra support or accommodation. That is the essence of equity in the workplace.

TEAM NORMS ARE WELL-DEFINED AND FOLLOWED

I am always amazed by how many organizations do not establish and document norms or ways of working. There is often an assumption that everyone knows the culture and that the norms are part of that. But often the norms are unspoken, and the assumption is everyone will learn them through observation. Unfortunately, this does not always happen, and many times without norms, you perpetuate old bad habits that need to be changed for DEI to be successful.

Team norms guide how we will all work together. They capture the principles we want all employees to operate under and become agreements on how we will all conduct ourselves at work. Well-defined norms create consistent and positive interpersonal interactions and help everyone work productively toward a common goal. They are a great place to incorporate elements of psychological safety.

Team norms focus on expected behaviors at work. To reinforce that, positive behaviors are celebrated, and negative behaviors are addressed in a timely and respectful manner. Norms may vary from team to team based on the kind of work each team does, but they will all align with the organization's mission and values. It is part of how those are lived out every day at work.

Some team norms may seem like obvious behaviors that every employee should know to do, but until you document and communicate them, you cannot hold employees accountable for them. Setting clear expectations for behavior builds a strong foundation for operationalizing DEI and embedding it into all the ways your employees work together.

KEY TAKEAWAYS

- Leverage data and analytics to identify your DEI opportunities.
- Define accountability for DEI for every leader.
- Cascade DEI education down to all of your employees so everyone has a common understanding of the key concepts and language.

- Communicate, communicate, communicate!
- Develop employee lifecycles and empathy maps to make all of your policies, benefits, and processes equitable and inclusive.
- Create ERGs for employees with shared identities to engage with each other, and for allies to learn how to best support those employees.
- Celebrate, celebrate, celebrate!
- Do not move forward with your DEI plans unless you have active listening, open communication, coaching, and development well ingrained in your organization, as well as clear and consistently followed team norms that reinforce inclusive and equitable behaviors.

CHAPTER 6

EXPANDING AND ENHANCING DEI

Congratulations! If you are at this point in your DEI journey, you have done the hard work of defining your DEI goals and strategy, building a strong foundation for the work, and integrating DEI into all the ways of working at your organization. Now, you get to focus on expanding and enhancing your DEI work so you can achieve maximum impact year over year.

This is also where you get to build out your external DEI efforts in a more formal and robust fashion. As I mentioned earlier, many organizations will choose elements from all three pillars of the Equity At Work™ Maturity Model to start with, rather than starting only with the activities in the first pillar before moving to the second and then the third. This is completely fine as long as you address everything in each pillar, plus the cultural requirements, before fully moving to the next one. You may have already had some community outreach or a supplier diversity program in place before getting to this stage of the model. That is okay! This is the step where you get to review that in more detail and build out the elements that will make it fully align with your DEI strategy, goals, and operations.

The rationale for holding the external work to this third pillar is that, typically, organizations have a fair amount of work to do to get their internal house in order, and I like that to be in solid shape before diving deeply into external work. This communicates to your employees that you are prioritizing their experience and addressing their needs before getting too focused externally. It will also help prevent you from developing an external approach that isn't well aligned with your internal approach and work.

In this final pillar, we will tackle the final stages of expanding accountability, communications, and education internally; building out your external DEI work; and establishing a process for continuous improvement.

Expanding & Enhancing DEI

Include DEI success measures in all leadership performance reviews

Include contribution toward DEI goals in all employee performance plans

Equip leaders with a playbook for addressing DEI current events

Embed DEI in all key internal and external communications and events

Continually invest in DEI education

Define supplier diversity, establish goals, and track spending

Develop and launch community outreach and external partnerships that align with DEI goals

Share learnings and best practices across the organization

Essential DEI Steps

Inclusive Leadership Style

Culture of Transparency

Culture Requirements

INCLUDE DEI SUCCESS MEASURES IN ALL LEADERSHIP PERFORMANCE REVIEWS

In the last chapter, we covered how to establish accountability among senior leaders for DEI work. At this stage, it is time to cascade that accountability down to all leaders.

Remember, when thinking through accountability, there are four aspects to consider:

1. Who the owner is, specifically who is in charge of directing the work even if this is not who will do the work.

2. What specific aspects of DEI they are responsible for, which can be solving a specific issue, launching a program, or something else.

3. What goals, both quantitative and qualitative, they are responsible for achieving.

4. How ownership will be measured in their performance review, including the impact on their raise and bonus.

As you cascade your goals down from senior leadership to all leaders, the goals within each department or business unit should work together to achieve the overall goals for that part of the organization. Let's say turnover is a big issue within the finance department, and the CFO has goals related to improving engagement and retention. The leaders who report to the CFO will have goals aimed at improving engagement and retention, but they will be focused on specific actions or activities. Engagement goals could break out into mentorship, team-building activities, and ERG membership, divided across three leaders in the CFO's organization.

Retention may break out into providing updated materials and talking points to recruiters, a review of exit interviews for common themes, and research into what competitors are doing to retain finance employees, again divided across three leaders in the organization.

It is important here to identify goals that leaders can directly influence. Making goals SMART—Specific, Measurable, Achievable, Realistic, and Time-bound—is a great way to ensure a leader can get them done within the time provided. Identifying partners and dependencies, whether they be people, budget, access to information, or something else, will also ensure the goal can be met. A little diligence here goes a long way. Monthly check-ins and read-outs to the whole team will also help everyone stay up to date on progress, brainstorm how to work through any issues, and provide visibility to progress so there are no surprises at the end of the year.

INCLUDE CONTRIBUTION TOWARD DEI GOALS IN ALL EMPLOYEE PERFORMANCE PLANS

To me, this is a really exciting step because you are giving everyone a role to play in making DEI part of the DNA of your organization. Below the leader level, these goals can be focused on participation, advocacy, sharing ideas, helping to organize, and other support needs. I have yet to come across an organization where the majority of employees are not excited to get involved in DEI work, as inclusion tends to be something most people like to rally around. The key thing to remember here is to make sure what you are asking of employees is manageable with their other work responsibilities. If they are stretched, help them determine how to prioritize all the things on their plates and adjust their goals accordingly.

This is where the work becomes fully inclusive since everyone is contributing to the progress of the entire organization. Some of the best ideas come from your junior employees since they are not stuck in old habits or old ways of working. Be sure to create space for listening and brainstorming so you can capture and test their ideas.

EQUIP LEADERS WITH A PLAYBOOK FOR ADDRESSING DEI CURRENT EVENTS

An area where a lot of organizations get tripped up is which social issues to weigh in on related to DEI. I outlined a number of recommendations regarding communications in the last chapter, and those still apply here. The difference is in providing specific guidance to all leaders, so you will be extending ownership of messaging beyond a centralized or corporate communications team so that leaders can be the voice for their teams on current events. Centralized communications can go through these steps as well, but some events may be local to only one location, and that is when it is important for the local leader on the front lines to be equipped to handle questions and manage expectations about what current events will be addressed and how. A simple playbook for how to address DEI current events and social issues goes a long way here. Ultimately, the key is for the decision on what to weigh in on make logical sense, be consistent across issues, and be consistent internally and externally.

Here are some questions you can use to help you develop standards for what issues you will weigh in on:

1. Does this directly impact our business, employees, and/or business partners?

2. Does weighing in on this issue align with our strategy and values? Does NOT weighing in go against our strategy and values?

3. Does weighing in on this issue align with our employee promise and/or value proposition?

4. Will weighing in help us serve our customers, communities, investors, and/or industry?

5. Will weighing in impact our reputation positively, negatively, or not at all? If our reputation could be negatively impacted, and we still feel this is important, how can we best prepare for that response?

6. Can we drive change on this issue? If so, are there others we should collaborate with proactively in alignment with our response?

Whether you use these questions or develop your own, working through them like a decision tree will provide an easy guide for what to communicate. Then you can develop communication plans and feedback plans as outlined in the last chapter. Once you develop your standards, sharing those internally will help employees trust that the organization has taken the time to be thoughtful about what to weigh in on.

EMBED DEI IN ALL KEY INTERNAL AND EXTERNAL COMMUNICATIONS AND EVENTS

This step takes your communications plans and feedback loops to the next level, having all relevant communications include a tie to your DEI mission and goals. Similar to constantly referencing your values and how your work enables you to live those out, connecting the dots between your DEI objectives and the ways you are investing in them demonstrates the depth of your commitment and how it is part of your organization's DNA.

This does not mean you need to incessantly beat the drum about DEI at every turn. Instead, this is about making sure you are intentionally referencing how the things you are doing are engendering inclusion and belonging, ensuring fairness, and celebrating all the great benefits that a diverse workforce brings wherever appropriate. It is much more about demonstrating how you are living out the principles of DEI than using the term DEI over and over.

Beyond communications, team-building activities and corporate events can also present opportunities to incorporate DEI. You can include fun DEI-related games and activities and use pictures and videos to tell stories that reinforce your principles. These are great to include in recruiting, onboarding, training, website, and social media material.

CONTINUALLY INVEST IN DEI EDUCATION

DEI training is not a one-time event. As you progress in your maturity, you can bring in more nuanced, behavioral topics that help people understand how to live out the DEI values you have identified as most important to your organization. Weaving these into standard leadership training is as important as providing standalone DEI training, which can come in many forms: self-directed, lunch and learns, speakers, book clubs, and formal sessions.

Revisit the table of topics in the last chapter for a refresher on ideas for what to include here. If you experienced resistance to any of the steps in setting your foundation or operationalizing DEI, those could be prompts for you to dive deeper and determine if any training can help. The most common training content I see at this phase is geared toward helping people, especially mid-level leaders, develop and inclusively support their teams.

Those topics include:

- How to give coaching-based feedback that helps employees create more inclusion and combat bias
- How to live out DEI-oriented team norms in times of conflict and crisis
- How to differentiate between beliefs and behaviors and set clear expectations around workplace behaviors
- Deeper dives into psychological safety and how to work through barriers to psychological safety
- Bringing DEI principles into employee relations practices and reporting
- Building a trauma-informed workplace to establish a mentally healthy work environment
- Integrating empathy mapping into all employee-facing communications and process development
- Establishing DEI-based norms for working with colleagues and partners outside your organization

It is important to provide a variety of ways for employees to learn and practice these new skills and behaviors. Using a blend of in-person, remote, and self-directed methods will ensure that different learning styles and schedules can be accommodated. I also highly encourage you to incorporate reading, videos, and breakouts for discussion into your approach because that will provide different ways for your messages to hit home. My team has even developed word searches, matching games, a Jeopardy game, and other engagement tools to have some creative ways to engage with DEI content.

Remember, education does not have to come only in the form of formal training. It can include helpful hints in newsletters, a site on your internal portal with resources, content shared by ERGs, and more. Mixing it up will keep it fresh and interesting for your employees, and having it come from different parts of the organization helps to ensure it is getting embedded all around. One of our clients runs contests and gives awards to those who have learned the most from different educational pieces. That creates a lot of engagement and makes learning fun.

There is no definitive list of what to include here. Ultimately, your DEI education, training, and content need to be specific to your organization's culture and needs. This step will help you continually evolve your organization toward your ideal future state. Don't hesitate to identify any topic you think can help get you there.

DEFINE SUPPLIER DIVERSITY, ESTABLISH GOALS, AND TRACK SPENDING

Being intentional about your spending with suppliers—for materials and servicescan create opportunities to extend your DEI focus externally.

There are six key areas to consider when incorporating DEI into your supplier strategy:

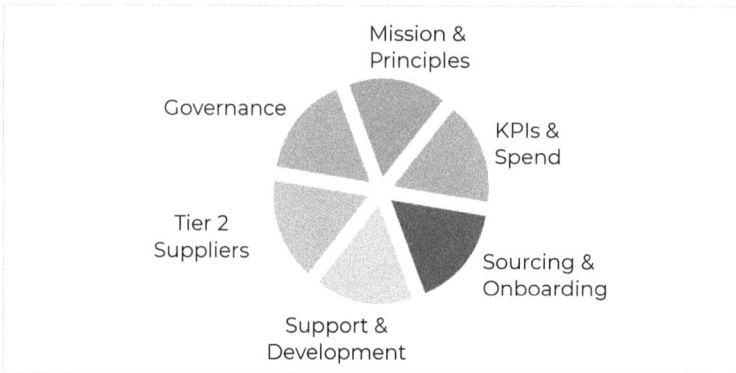

Mission &
Principles

Leading Practices:

➤ The definition of a diverse supplier is evolving beyond minority- and women-owned and operated businesses to include LGBTQ+, veteran, and disabled owned companies, as well as local small businesses

➤ Alignment of mission and values, especially related to DEI, is becoming increasingly important in selecting diverse supplier partners

➤ Striking a balance between centralized procurement and localized supplier decisions enables large companies to meet the unique needs of local communities and makes a bigger local impact

➤ Supplier diversity is part of a broader movement within the Environmental, Social and Governance (ESG) space where stakeholders are demanding more data and transparency on impact rather than just practices

KPIs & Spend	**Leading Practices:** ➤ Measure spend in both dollar amounts and % of total spend, as well as the amount and % of suppliers who are diverse within each category of spend ➤ Percentages offer a greater level of standardization across companies, industries, and time, while dollar amounts and raw numbers provide visibility into the specific impact being made ➤ Tracking and reporting spend at the sub-category level helps businesses set strategic spend goals that are both top-down and bottom-up and therefore more realistic
Sourcing & Onboarding	**Leading Practices:** ➤ Consideration of DEI when selecting service providers, i.e., law, accounting, and consulting firms, as well as suppliers of products and materials, is gaining traction and is a way for companies of any size to extend the reach of their DEI work ➤ Outreach efforts to source diverse suppliers include participating in supplier diversity fairs, joining national affinity groups and their regional chapters, and connecting with local chambers of commerce ➤ Using certified diverse suppliers helps qualify and promote diverse suppliers, but leaders are starting to understand the limitations of requiring certification from the outset. Some are partnering with suppliers to complete the certification process.

Support & Development

Leading Practices:

➤ Leading supplier diversity development programs extend the business relationship to incorporate executive coaching, training, and helping to build the suppliers' capabilities and capacity

➤ One of the biggest challenges minority-owned businesses face is access to working capital.   To combat this, companies are offering early payment programs to qualified diverse suppliers.

➤ Centralized vendor portals enable organizations to create searchable directories of diverse suppliers and increase visibility to diverse suppliers across the organization

Tier 2 Suppliers

Leading Practices:

➤ Organizations are increasing their commitment to building out a fully diverse supply chain by encouraging and in some cases requiring their direct (Tier 1) contracted suppliers to subcontract with diverse indirect (Tier 2) suppliers

➤ Ideally, these Tier 2 suppliers are not only diverse in ownership and internal workforce representation but also DEI-focused in their workplace values

➤ Reporting on supplier diversity is evolving to include measurements capturing both Tier 1 and Tier 2 spend, especially for global companies with significant spend on diverse suppliers

Governance   **Leading Practices:**

➤ Internal reporting that includes progress against diverse supplier spend goals creates accountability and spurs creative thinking on how to expand the program

➤ Leaders are discussing standardization of supplier diversity metrics to alleviate some of the burden on small suppliers to track, gather, and report on different data points requested by each of their clients

There are many organizations that can help you with your supplier diversity programs and goals, primarily by connecting you with certified businesses. Several of major organizations are listed below. You can also contact your local chambers of commerce for more information and local resources.

KEY ASSOCIATIONS & ORGANIZATIONS	
Billion Dollar Roundtable	The National Minority Supplier Development Council
Disability IN	US Hispanic Chamber of Commerce
National Center for American Indian Enterprise Development	U.S. Department of Commerce's Minority Business Development Agency
National Veteran Business Development Council	The National Gay and Lesbian Chamber of Commerce US
The Chartered Institute of Procurement and Supply	Women's Business Enterprise National Council
Pan Asian American Chamber of Commerce Education Foundation	·Local government agencies, chambers of commerce & institutes of higher education

DEVELOP AND LAUNCH COMMUNITY OUTREACH & EXTERNAL PARTNERSHIPS THAT ALIGN WITH DEI GOALS

Remember this framework from earlier?

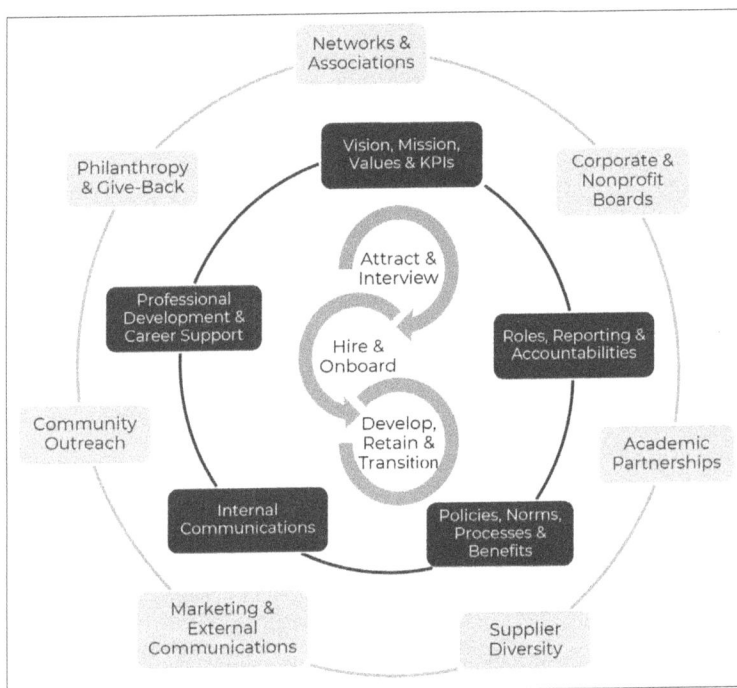

We are now in the outer ring of the framework, and this step is where you will think through opportunities to connect or partner with the following:

- Networks and Associations

  These can be industry or demographic-based (sometimes both) and typically include a combination of networking, professional development, advocacy, lobbying, and/or community service. They are wonderful to tap into because they have specific missions and can therefore have a captive audience that aligns with your DEI mission, creating an opportunity to expand your impact quickly. These groups are often looking for corporate sponsors, which can provide visibility and leadership opportunities. Even if you cannot or do not want to be a sponsor, you can still have one or many employees become members and join forces to have a bigger impact.

- Corporate and Nonprofit Boards

  You may have leaders in your organization currently serving on boards of directors of other organizations, both corporate and nonprofit. These can provide another opportunity for partnership and a joining of forces around a shared goal. Start by identifying who in your organization is filling these roles externally and then meet with them to see what opportunities exist around common goals related to DEI. If you do not have anyone currently filling one of these roles, you may identify a nonprofit organization that is aligned with your mission for DEI and see if anyone in your organization is willing to get involved. It may take some time for a Board seat to come open, so be patient if that is the case. There may also be requirements for how much time someone needs to be a member of that nonprofit or how much time or money they contribute to become a Board member, so be sure to do research on that before jumping in. Also, some organizations will sponsor a Board seat and then rotate members through that seat over the years. That can be a great way to develop a long-term partnership while enabling multiple people to participate in that role.

- Academic Partnerships

  These partnerships can extend beyond recruiting as a way to have a larger impact at some of the schools you partner with. Some of the most common actions here are sponsoring a committee or event on campus, running an internship program, doing career coaching, and sponsoring clubs and associations on campus that are related to your DEI goals. These partnerships are best done with a multi-year view and commitment so you can have a significant impact and gain insight into some of the biggest needs of these communities of students, professors, and administrators.

- Community Outreach

  Many of our clients engage in community outreach as a way to be directly involved in supporting people in the communities where they have offices and facilities. Community outreach is focused on longer-term partnerships or year-over-year events that do something to lift up those communities. It can take a variety of forms, from involvement in the local chambers of commerce to developing a partnership with a local nonprofit or community center. Let's say health equity is an area of focus for your DEI work; you could hold or sponsor an annual blood drive or pop-up diabetes screening and education clinic in your communities. Maybe you are a sports organization, and equitable access to sports and fitness is one of your DEI focus areas. You could sponsor a local school team that needs new equipment and uniforms and possibly even provide coaching.

- Philanthropy and Give-Back

  Philanthropy and give-back are also great ways to have an impact in your local communities through fundraising, donations, and volunteer hours. These can be ongoing commitments or shorter-term. Often, our clients will rotate what they donate to and volunteer for so that they cover a diverse set of needs in the community. Activities here range from backpack drives to food drives to walk-a-thons to cash and product donations. These are great ways to create social events that include employees from different functions and levels, which can break down barriers and create new connections within your organization.

SHARE LEARNINGS AND BEST PRACTICES ACROSS THE ORGANIZATION

As you continue to mature in your DEI work, you will develop your own best practices and learn many lessons along your journey. Sharing these across your organization will ensure everyone benefits from each other's learnings and work.

There are many ways to do this:

- Hold an ERG forum for ERG leaders
- Convene DEI leads from each department or division
- Develop a survey
- Hold focus groups
- Gather feedback through one to two specific questions in your engagement survey

You will also need to regularly revisit your roadmap, pivot as needed, and incorporate new ideas into upcoming plans.

Having a formal annual process in place to review the goals for the past year, what you achieved, where you encountered barriers, and what you want to plan next is important to keep the work focused on outcomes. This will naturally help you maintain momentum.

Finally, this can be a great step to bring in an outside facilitator or inspirational DEI speaker to help generate new ideas that you may not have thought of internally. DEI speakers typically have stories to share about being in the trenches in their own organizations or with clients. You can learn a lot from these, so it is a worthwhile investment of time and budget.

Now that we've covered the essential steps for "Operationalizing DEI," let's review the key cultural dependencies you need to have in place at this stage for your investment in DEI to work.

INCLUSIVE LEADERSHIP STYLE

An inclusive leadership style is directly connected to psychological safety and seeks to bring many different perspectives to decision-making. This does not mean the leader defaults to consensus; rather, the leader provides direction and guidance after soliciting and considering different points of view.

The actions a leader takes that make their style inclusive include:

- Building interpersonal trust—being honest and transparent, following through, establishing rapport by finding common ground, and valuing different perspectives

- Applying an adaptive mindset—taking a broad view, seeking to apply multiple perspectives, and adapting your approach to each situation

- Optimizing individual talent—supporting growth based on individual strengths and opportunities, motivating others, and joining forces for collective success across differences

- Staying strong in your commitment to inclusion—being willing to address difficult topics, bringing people of all backgrounds along the journey together, and aligning inclusion with business goals to keep commitments on track

There are five traits that are common among inclusive leaders. If these do not come naturally to you, do not worry, you can build these skills through coaching and practice.

TRAIT	REQUIREMENT
Authenticity	Vulnerability Humility
Emotional Resilience	Composure Not Taking Things Too Personally
Inquisitiveness	Curiosity Empathy
Optimism	Opportunity Mindset Confidence We Can Find Common Ground
Flexibility	Ability to Tolerate Ambiguity Adaptability

I find that many leaders who are Gen Xers or older have to be particularly intentional about adopting this style since it was not what was expected or rewarded as they came up the ranks as leaders. For leaders in highly operational, task-oriented roles where work tends to be very linear, this can also be the case. It is vital to invest in leadership development here so leaders can role-model inclusion from the top.

CULTURE OF TRANSPARENCY

A culture of transparency is one in which sharing information is the norm so that everyone has visibility into plans, progress, learnings, hurdles, and performance. This does not mean everything is shared with everyone. Instead, information is at an appropriate level of detail for each level in the organization. The difference from a more traditional culture is the information is shared below leadership levels to all employees, and likely also includes strategic partners. This helps everyone feel like they are "in it" together and working toward common goals. It also goes a long way toward building trust across the organization because employees feel they understand the purpose of what they and others are asked to do.

Like an inclusive leadership style, a culture of transparency is directly related to psychological safety. Here, employees are encouraged and able to ask questions, make suggestions, and raise concerns, and lessons from those discussions are shared across the organization for everyone's benefit. At this stage of DEI maturity, this is critical to continuous improvement because it sets the stage for open discussion and sharing of ideas.

KEY TAKEAWAYS

- Every employee has an opportunity to contribute to DEI work

- DEI needs to be embedded in internal and external communications, with leaders having a playbook for how to develop talking points on current events

- DEI education should be an ongoing investment

- Supplier diversity, community outreach, and external partnerships are all opportunities to extend your DEI goals and principles outside of your organization

- Sharing teachings and best practices across your organization will ensure continuous improvement and help you develop your own best practices

- Focusing leaders on developing an inclusive style will help employees feel heard and valued while role-modeling desired inclusive behaviors

- Establishing a culture of transparency builds trust and helps everyone feel like they are clear on the purpose of their work

CHAPTER 7

BEST PRACTICES AND MANAGING RESISTANCE

Congratulations! You have made it through all the stages of DEI maturity! Now it is time to share some overarching guidance on best practices and how to keep your organization moving forward throughout its journey.

BEST PRACTICES

To set the stage for thinking about best practices, I want to first focus on the mindset that works best related to this work. There are four key elements to remember here:

1. Recognize that DEI is about behavior and values, not just policy and process

2. Acknowledge this is a journey, for each of us individually and the organization in total

3. Be transparent about what is working, what is not, and what we're going to do about it

4. Lean into empathy and role-model this for others

These should all sound familiar, as these principles are woven throughout the book. Reinforcing these elements in all of your DEI planning communications will help everyone embed them in your work.

The following best practices are learnings from all of my years of doing DEI work, both as part of non-DEI leadership roles and as a DEI consultant to organizations of all shapes and sizes. They are my tried-and-true methods that form the foundation of all of Equity At Work™'s work.

EQUITY AT WORK™ TOP TEN DEI BEST PRACTICES

1. **Lead by listening** in a way that demonstrates empathy, giving everyone space to be heard respectfully, playing back what you heard, and then being clear about how that will or will not be incorporated into your plans, either now or in the future, and why

2. **Be honest** about where you are today, where you want to go, what it is going to take to get there, and what is standing in your way

3. Develop your DEI strategy in a **culture-specific way**, starting by defining what D, E, and I mean at your organization, aligning it with your vision, mission, and values, and determining how it enables you to live out your promises to your employees, partners, customers, and communities

4. Be crystal clear about the **purpose of the work**, whether it be to solve a problem, provide education, enable advocacy, or something else

5. **Set goals for both internal and external DEI work** based on your honest assessment and aligned with the purpose of your work. Determine how to pace going after those goals in alignment with your other organizational priorities. Resource and run it like a complex program.

6. **Be real or don't do DEI work at all.** If anything you are doing, training, or saying is performative, STOP.

7. **Operationalize DEI**, integrating it into all of your normal ways of working so it becomes part of your organization's DNA

8. Make sure your **CEO leads this work from the front** and role-model this for others

9. Create **clear, specific accountability** for DEI for every person in a people leader role

10. **Ground your DEI work in change management** by defining and communicating "What is in it for me?" focusing on behavioral change, and providing visibility into plans, progress, learnings, and pivots

Following these best practices will enable you to effectively integrate DEI into every touchpoint with your employees, business, and community partners, and to mobilize all of your people leaders to accomplish this.

Ultimately, you will need to determine the best approach for your organization based on your culture, values, priorities, and how quickly you like to drive change. These best practices can help you develop your own framework for DEI.

Here is how we bring all of this together into our step-by-step approach to DEI work:

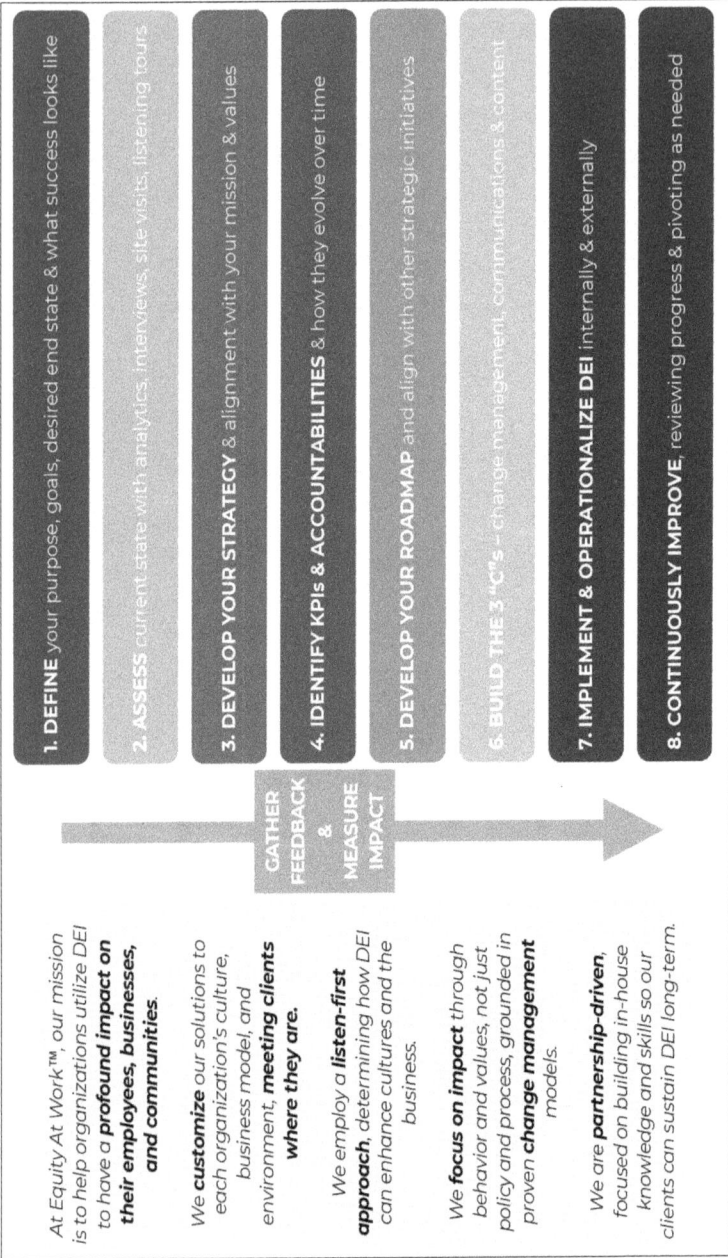

142   Do DEI Right

1. DEFINE your purpose, goals, desired end state & what success looks like

2. ASSESS current state with analytics, interviews, site visits, listening tours

3. DEVELOP YOUR STRATEGY & alignment with your mission & values

4. IDENTIFY KPIs & ACCOUNTABILITIES & how they evolve over time

5. DEVELOP YOUR ROADMAP and align with other strategic initiatives

6. BUILD THE 3 "C"s – change management, communications & content

7. IMPLEMENT & OPERATIONALIZE DEI internally & externally

8. CONTINUOUSLY IMPROVE, reviewing progress & pivoting as needed

GATHER FEEDBACK & MEASURE IMPACT

At Equity At Work™, our mission is to help organizations utilize DEI to have a *profound impact on their employees, businesses, and communities.*

We *customize* our solutions to each organization's culture, business model, and environment, *meeting clients where they are.*

We employ a *listen-first approach*, determining how DEI can enhance cultures and the business.

We *focus on impact* through behavior and values, not just policy and process, grounded in proven *change management* models.

We are *partnership-driven*, focused on building in-house knowledge and skills so our clients can sustain DEI long-term.

Scan the QR code to learn more
about our approach:

HANDLING RESISTANCE TO CHANGE

Many organizations that have made statements in support of DEI can still be slow to make progress. Leadership may be misaligned, other priorities may be competing for attention, and work can be delegated to people who can't drive decisions.

This resistance to change, whether intentional or not, is one of the biggest issues my clients face. It can come in direct forms but more often is passive and indirect.

Here are three common examples:

1. The issue is delegated to ERGs to solve—and yet ERGs are typically comprised primarily of more junior-level employees who are the ones facing the problem in the first place, and they don't have the power or access to drive real change.

2. There is little to no resourcing—because DEI is not historically a standing line item on a P&L, leaders often ask those passionate about driving change to take the lead and do the best they can with what they have (which usually means doing this as a side project on top of their full-time job, with no budget and no extra pay).

3. The goal is just to "do better"—if you do not know what you are aiming for, it is virtually impossible to be successful in making meaningful, positive change happen.

I do not think these actions are taken to intentionally slow anything down. Most leaders and employees genuinely want DEI work to make a positive difference in their organizations. So what is behind this?

Many times, it comes down to a lack of alignment and prioritization at the top—which is really the rigor of making DEI a strategic priority. Leadership may be aligned on the sentiment behind DEI but not on how to go about driving change. In addition, there is often a fear of what will be uncovered as the work gets underway. What if there is a deeper issue at play, or the change is so systemic that we need to overhaul the way we have always worked? Combine misalignment, uncertainty about how to move forward, and fear of what may come, and you have a perfect formula for stalling out.

So how can you break down this resistance and make positive DEI change happen now?

- Get grounded in the pain points DEI issues are causing the business, both in terms of performance and in terms of people. Are you losing clients? Investors? Key talent? These are things leaders are measured on regularly and highly incentivized to fix if broken.

- Articulate exactly what you mean by DEI. How do diversity, equity, and inclusion align with your core values, culture, and business proposition? How will customers, shareholders, and employees experience them in their interactions with your company?

- Make DEI a standing agenda item on all town hall and leadership team meetings. Do regular reporting on actions, learnings, progress, upcoming events, and ways to get involved. Keep DEI top of mind and highly accessible.

- Incorporate allyship into your DEI approach at every turn. Ask influential, passionate employees at all levels to get involved and advocate on your behalf. Use DEI meetings and events as opportunities to educate and inform everyone so they can all be part of the solution planning and delivery.

- Set measurable goals and say them OUT LOUD. Publish them, track progress against them, share what you learn, and pivot if needed. Make sure they are both ambitious and grounded in the reality of where you are starting. Align resources to make the most important goals highly achievable.

- Remember that small acts add up to big change. Storytelling is a powerful tool here. Highlight the changes that made a real difference to an employee, in getting a new client, or in anticipating a customer's need. This will create tremendous momentum.

DEI change is not up to any one of us. Rather, it is up to all of us. Partnership is at the core of all of this work, starting at the very top. If you sense DEI is a solo mission in your organization, that is a clear sign that resistance is in play, and it is time to use the steps above to intervene.

RESPONDING TO PUSHBACK ON DEI

Understand that most pushback on DEI comes from a place of fear, whether the person resisting realizes it or not. This fear is usually tied to a concern that giving more to someone else necessitates taking away from them or people like them. It can also come from a worry that they may discover they have been complicit in a system that has kept others down. Finally, it can be related to a concern that the system they have mastered will have to change, which may result in them not doing as well in the new system. This, in turn, could impact their comfort level, their way of working, and possibly their compensation.

Regardless of the reason, if you are sensing pushback, you must face it head-on. If you do not, you risk being undermined behind the scenes, and you will not be able to go far with your work. Creating spaces to listen and engage in conversation about what the concerns are, and how they can potentially be mitigated, will help you keep moving forward. As with any initiative, it will be impossible to make everyone happy, but you can ensure they feel heard.

Here are tips for addressing pushback and concerns. If you feel like you are in over your head, don't hesitate to bring in a leader and/or HR.

> - Pause
> - Be open to **dialogue**
> - Actively **listen** to concerns
> - **Validate** by playing back what you heard and asking if that is correct
> - Correct any misconceptions or misinformation with **facts**
> - **Thank them** for sharing their concerns
> - Discuss how DEI work helps us live out our **company mission and values**
> - **Share stories** that demonstrate the benefits and positive impacts of DEI
> - Find ways for them to be **included in the work**
> - **Escalate** if you feel uncomfortable or ill-equipped

KEY TAKEAWAYS

- The best practices in DEI work are grounded in listening, empathy, honesty, and being purpose-driven
- DEI work needs to be defined to fit your culture, mission, and values, and incorporate internal and external goals
- Leaders need to lead from the front, be transparent, and utilize a change-management-driven approach
- DEI should ultimately be part of your DNA, integrated into all the ways you connect with your employees, business, communities, and partners
- Resistance to DEI can come from an overall resistance to change or something deeper, typically fear
- Create space to listen and have a dialogue about any concerns related to DEI

CHAPTER 8

LET'S GET TO IT!

D EI work presents a tremendous opportunity for companies to demonstrate how they will show up for all of their
stakeholders on issues—employees, board members, stock-
holders, and the public at large. Not just talk but taking action
internally, with customers, and in the community. Is this the
catalyst that makes you dig in and re-evaluate your hiring and
promotion processes? Or jointly participate in an industry task
force with clients? Or engage in nonprofit work that directly
impacts your community?

Ultimately, DEI is about focusing on your people and
ensuring they are all set up to achieve their full potential in
your organization. DEI is not about handouts or taking from
one person to give to another. Instead, it is about ensuring
everyone has an opportunity to succeed as their full, authentic
selves, free of code-switching, hiding parts of our lives, and
pretending we are okay with inequitable treatment.

We need work to be a haven for all of us. We give so much
to work—the majority of our waking hours, our thinking, our
creativity, our ideas, our team members' development, and

more—that we need our employers to support us meaningfully. Many employers are working hard to evolve and provide benefits and services that are in tune with what today's workforce really needs, including flexible schedules, mental health services, financial planning support, parental leave, and more. But this is inconsistent and typically limited to very large organizations and even then to corporate employees and not the hourly workforce.

DEI bridges these gaps because at its core, DEI is about meeting all of your employees where they are and providing them the tools, systems, processes, policies, and benefits so they can all be set up for success. Focusing on DEI ensures everyone can feel seen, heard, and valued for who they are and feel confident that they can contribute and develop to their fullest extent. That there is no need to pretend to be someone else or try to fit an outdated model to progress in their careers. That there are varied paths to advancement that match the varied capabilities and contributions of employees.

Companies and employees both win when they focus on DEI. Employees are more engaged, productive, and loyal to a DEI-centric company. DEI-focused companies outpace those that are not in revenue, profit, return on invested capital, innovation, and capturing new markets. Business partners, suppliers, and vendors benefit because the principles and values of DEI are extended to them. The communities these companies and employees are located in benefit because the external efforts of a DEI-centric organization apply the same lens to community outreach, philanthropy, and giving back. DEI creates a huge win all around.

So get to it! Even if you start small, you will create a ripple effect that works its way around your organization and sows the seeds of change.

DEI HOLIDAYS
AND OBSERVANCES CALENDAR

At Equity At Work™, one of the many resources that we have created for clients is a DEI Holidays and Observances Calendar. Here is a copy for you to use for your planning.

EQUITY

DEI HOLIDAYS AND OBSERVANCES CALENDAR

Observance	Date	Observed by...	Observed (in)...	About
Last Day of Kwanzaa	January 1	African-Americans, Africans	Worldwide	Observed by African-American and Black communitites, the end of Kwanzaa is a time to reflect on collective purpose and unity with a feast (Karamu), candle lighting, and cultural activities.
World Braille Day	January 4	Everyone	Worldwide	Observed by disability and accessibility advocates worldwide, World Braille Day is observed to honor Louis Braille's birthday and raise awareness about blind and visually impaired rights.
Eastern Orthodox Christmas	January 7	Eastern Orthodox Christians	Worldwide	Observed by Eastern Orthodox Christians in countries like Russia, Serbia, and Ethiopia, Eastern Orthodox Christmas celebrates the Nativity of Christ with liturgical services, fasting, and traditional meals.
Bodhi Day	January 10	Mahāyāna Buddhists	Worldwide	Observed by Mahayana Buddhists, primarily in East Asia, Bodhi Day marks the Buddha's enlightenment under the Bodhi tree with meditation, chanting, and acts of kindness.
Orthodox New Year	January 14	Orthodox Christians / Eastern Europeans / Russians	Worldwide, primarily in Eastern Europe and Russia	Observed by Eastern Orthodox Christians using the Julian calendar in Eastern Europe, the Orthodox New Year is celebrated with church services and cultural festivities.
Makar Sankranti	January 14 (15 on leap yrs)	Hindus	Worldwide, primarily in South Asia	Observed by Hindus in India and Nepal, Makar Sankranti marks the sun's transition into Capricorn and the harvest and is celebrated with with kite flying, sweets, and rituals.
Tu Bishvat / Rosh HaShanah La'Ilanot	Varies - Typically January or February (Fifteenth Day of Shevat)	Jewish People	Worldwide	Observed by Jews worldwide, especially in Israel, Tu Bishvat is the "New Year for Trees" and is celebrated with tree planting and special meals featuring fruits and nuts.
Martin Luther King Jr. Day	Third Monday in January	Everyone	U.S.	Observed in the United States, Martin Luther King Jr. Day honors the civil rights leader's legacy of nonviolent activism through service projects and educational programs.
International Holocaust Remembrance Day	January 27	Everyone	Worldwide	Observed globally, International Holocaust Remembrance Day honors the victims of the Holocaust and reaffirms the commitment to never forget this atrocity.
Lunar New Year	Begins between January 21 - February 20 (w/ the 1st new moon of the lunar calendar). Ends 15 days later (w/ the 1st full moon)	Chinese, Vietnamese, Korean, Tibetan and other Asian/AAPI communities	Worldwide, among many Asian communities	Observed by East and Southeast Asian cultures, the Lunar New Year marks the start of the lunar calendar year and is celebrated with family reunions, dances, and red envelopes.
Black History Month	February	Everyone	U.S.	Observed in the U.S. and Canada (February) and the UK (October), Black History Month honors African diasporic history and achievements.
Parinirvana	February 15	Mahāyāna Buddhists	Worldwide	Observed by Mahayana Buddhists, Parinirvana commemorates the Buddha's death and entry into final Nirvana and is observed with temple visits, meditation, and reflection on impermanence.
Maha Shiravatri	February or March (the 14th night of the dark half of the Hindu month of Phalguna)	Hindus	Worldwide	Observed by Hindus globally, Maha Shiravatri honors Lord Shiva through night-long vigils, fasting, and temple rituals.

Lailat al Miraj	27th night of the Islamic month of Rajab	Muslims	Worldwide	Observed by Muslims worldwide, Lailat al Miraj commemorates the Prophet Muhammad's night journey and ascension to heaven and is observed with prayers and storytelling.
Ash Wednesday	46 days before Easter, which is determined as the Sunday following the first full moon that happens on or after the March equinox on March 21	Christians	Worldwide	Observed by Western Christians, Ash Wednesday marks the beginning of Lent, a time of repentance, and it is observed by attending services and receiving ashes on the forehead.
National Women's History Month	March	Everyone	U.S.	Observed in the United States in March, National Women's History Month highlights women's contributions to history and society.
International Women's Day	March 8 in the US, Germany, Denmark, Austria and Switzerland; can be observed on any day of the year by UN Member States in accordance with their historical and national traditions	Everyone	Worldwide	Observed globally on March 8 to advocate for gender equality and celebrate women's achievements, with rallies, panels, and cultural programs.
AAPI Women's Equal Pay Day	This date symbolizes how far into the year AAPI women must work to earn what men earned in the previous year	Everyone	U.S.	Observed in the U.S., AAPI Women's Equal Pay Day raises awareness about the wage gap facing Asian American and Pacific Islander women.
Purim	Celebrated annually on the 14th day of the Hebrew month of Adar	Jewish People	Worldwide	Observed by Jews worldwide, Purim marks the biblical story of Esther's heroism and is celebrated with costumes, feasting, and reading the Megillah.
Holi	Twelfth month of Phalguna in the Hindu calendar. Typically March.	Hindus	Worldwide	Observed by Hindus in India and worldwide, Holi celebrates spring and the triumph of good over evil and is observed with colored powders, dancing, and festive music.
Hola Mohalla	Second day of the lunar month of Chett. Typically March	Sikhs	Worldwide	Observed by Sikhs in India. Hola Mohalla is a festival following Holi that features displays of martial arts, processions, and kirtan.
International Transgender Day of Visibility	March 31	Everyone	Worldwide	Observed globally, International Transgender Day of Visibility celebrates trans and nonbinary people and raises awareness around violence and discrimination targeting trans people.
World Autism Month	April	Everyone	Worldwide	Observed globally in April, World Autism Month promotes awareness, acceptance, and understanding of autism.
Ramadan	Ninth month of the Islamic calendar	Muslims	Worldwide	Observed by Muslims worldwide, Ramadan is a holy month of fasting, prayer, and reflection to commemorate the Qur'an's revelation.
World Autism Awareness Day	April 2	Everyone	Worldwide	Observed global, World Autism Awareness Day fosters understanding and support for autistic individuals.
Vaisakhi	First day of the month of Vaisakha. Typically April 13 or 14	Sikhs and Punjabis	Worldwide	Observed by Sikhs and Hindus in India, Vaisakhi celebrates the harvest and the formation of Sikh Khalsa.
Passover / Pesach	From the 15th day of the Hebrew month of Nissan (or Nisan) through the 22nd day. Typically in March or April	Jewish People	Worldwide	Observed by Jews worldwide, Passover commemorates the Exodus from Egypt and is celebrated with a Seder, storytelling, and the removal of leavened food.

Good Friday	The Friday before Easter	Christians	Worldwide	Observed by Christians, Good Friday is a time to mourn Jesus's crucifixion and features solemn services, fasting, and scripture readings.
Easter	The first Sunday following the full Moon that occurs on or just after the spring equinox	Christians	Worldwide	Observed by Christians globally, Easter celebrates Jesus's resurrection and features church services and feasts.
National Equal Pay Day	This date symbolizes how far into the year women must work to earn what men earned in the previous year	Everyone	U.S.	Observed in the U.S., National Equal Pay Day highlights the gender pay gap, calculated as how far into the year women must work to earn what men did the previous year.
Day of Silence	Second Friday of April	Everyone	U.S.	Observed primarily in U.S. schools by LGBTQ+ students and allies, Day of Silence is an annual protest against bullying and discrimination.
Eastern Orthodox Holy Friday	Three days before the first Sunday following the full Moon that occurs after the vernal equinox using the Julian calendar. Typically April or May	Orthodox Christians	Worldwide	Observed by Orthodox Christians, Eastern Orthodox Holy Friday commemorates Christ's crucifixion with solemn liturgies and processions.
Eastern Orthodox Pascha (Easter)	The first Sunday following the full Moon that occurs after the vernal equinox using the Julian calendar. Typically April or May	Orthodox Christians	Worldwide	Observed by Orthodox Christians, Eastern Orthodox Pascha celebrates the resurrection of Christ with midnight services and traditional feasting.
23rd Night of Ramadan	23rd night of the month of Ramadan	Shia Muslims	Worldwide	Observed by Shia Muslims, the 23rd night of Ramadan is an especially sacred night for worship and forgiveness near the end of Ramadan and is observed with intensified prayer and Qur'an recitation.
27th Night of Ramadan	27th night of the month of Ramadan	Sunnis Muslims	Worldwide	Observed by Sunni Muslims, the 27th night of Ramadan is believed to be when the Qur'an was revealed and is marked by all-night prayer and supplication.
Eid al-Fitr	The first day after Ramadan	Muslims	Worldwide	Observed by Muslims worldwide, Eid al-Fitr marks the end of Ramadan and is celebrated with festive prayers, meals, and giving of charity (zakat al-fitr).
Asian American and Pacific Islander Heritage Month	May	Everyone	U.S.	Observed in the U.S., Asian American and Pacific Islander Heritage Month honors the contributions and achievements of Asian and Pacific Islander Americans.
International Day Against Homophobia, Transphobia and Biphobia	May 17	Everyone	Worldwide	Observed globally, International Day Against Homophobia, Transphobia, and Biphobia serves to combat LGBTQ+ discrimination with marches, education, and public campaigns.
Memorial Day	Last Monday of May	Everyone	U.S.	Observed in the U.S., Memorial Day honors military personnel who died in service and is marked by cemetery visits, parades, and national moments of remembrance.
Pride Month	June	Everyone	U.S.	Observed globally, Pride Month celebrates LGBTQ+ identities and history.
Eastern Orthodox Ascension Day	40 days after Pascha. Typically May or June	Orthodox Christians	Worldwide	Observed by Orthodox Christians, Eastern Orthodox Ascension Day commemorates Christ's ascension 40 days after Easter.

Shavuot	Seven weeks after Passover / Pesach. Typically May or June	Jewish People	Worldwide	Observed by Jews, Shavuot commemorates the receiving the Torah at Sinai.
Juneteenth	June 19	Everyone	U.S.	Observed in the U.S., Juneteenth commemorates the emancipation of enslaved African Americans and celebrates Black culture and achievement.
National Indigenous Peoples Day	June 21	Everyone	Canada	Observed in Canada on June 21, National Indigenous Peoples Day celebrates First Nations, Inuit, and Métis heritage.
Holy Day of Arafah	9th day of the 12th and final month of the lunar Islamic Calendar	Muslims	Worldwide	Observed by Muslims during Hajj, the Holy Day of Arafah is a day of prayer and fasting; pilgrims stand at Mount Arafat and non-pilgrims fast at home
Eid al-Adha	10th day of the 12th and final month of the lunar Islamic Calendar	Muslims	Worldwide	Observed by Muslims worldwide, Eid al-Adha commemorates Abraham's willingness to sacrifice his son and is celebrated with communal prayers, animal sacrifices, and charity.
International Non-Binary People's Day	July 14	Everyone	Worldwide	Observed globally, International Non-Binary Peoples Day is commemorated to recognize and uplift non-binary people.
Eid al-Ghadir	18th of Dhu al-Hijjah in the Islamic lunar calendar	Shia and Bektashi Muslims	Worldwide	Observed by Shia Muslims, Eid al-Ghadir marks the Prophet Muhammad's appointment of Ali as his successor.
National Disability Independence Day	July 26	Everyone	Worldwide	Observed in the U.S., National Disability Independence Day marks the signing of the Americans with Disabilities Act (ADA) in 1990.
1st of Muharram (Islamic New Year)	1st of Muharram, the first month in the Islamic calendar	Muslims	Worldwide	Observed by Muslims globally, the 1st of Muharram begins the Islamic calendar year.
Black Women's Equal Pay Day	This date symbolizes how far into the year Black women must work to earn what men earned in the previous year	Everyone	U.S.	Observed in the U.S., Black Women's Equal Pay Day highlights pay disparities facing Black women.
10th day of Muharram (Ashura)	The 10th day of the first month (Muharram) of the Islamic calendar	Muslims	Worldwide	Observed by Muslims for multiple reasons: for Sunni Muslims, this is a day of fasting; for Shia Muslims, this is a day to mourn the martyrdom of Husayn ibn Ali.
Women's Equality Day	August 26	Everyone	U.S.	Observed in the U.S., Women's Equality Day commemorates the 1920 certification of the 19th Amendment, which gave all American women the right to vote.
Native Women's Equal Pay Day	This date symbolizes how far into the year Native women must work to earn what men earned in the previous year	Everyone	U.S.	Observed in the U.S., Native Women's Equal Pay Day spotlights wage gaps faced by Native American women.
International Equal Pay Day	September 18	Everyone	Worldwide	Observed globally, International Equal Pay Day promotes pay equity across genders through international campaigns and policy advocacy.
National Hispanic Heritage Month	September 15 - October 15	Everyone	U.S.	Observed in the U.S., National Hispanic Heritage Month celebrates Hispanic and Latino contributions and achievements.

Rosh Hashanah	Beginning of the month of Tishrei. Typically in September or October	Jewish People	Worldwide	Observed by Jews worldwide, Rosh Hashanah is the Jewish New Year and is celebrated with prayer services, the blowing of the shofar, and festive meals.
Yom Kippur	Tenth day of the seventh month, Tishrei. Typically in September or October	Jewish People	Worldwide	Observed by Jews worldwide, Yom Kippur is the Day of Atonement and is marked by fasting, prayer, and reflection.
Mawlid	Commemorated primarily on 12th of Rabi' al-Awwal, the third month in the Islamic calendar, or the 17th by Shia Muslims	Muslims	Worldwide	Observed by Muslims, Mawlid celebrates the birth of Prophet Muhammad and features religious lectures, poetry, and community meals.
Sukkot	Begins 15th day of the month of Tishrei. Typically in September or October	Jewish People	Worldwide	Observed by Jews worldwide, Sukkot commemorates the Israelites' journey in the wilderness and is marked by dwelling in temporary huts (sukkot) and enjoying festive meals.
National Disability Employment Awareness Month	October	Everyone	U.S.	Observed in the U.S., National Disability Employment Awareness Month promotes inclusive hiring and celebrates the contributions of disabled workers.
World Mental Health Day	October 10	Everyone	Worldwide	Observed globally, World Mental Health Day raises awareness of mental health issues and advocates for increased services and inclusion.
Indigenous Peoples' Day	Second Monday in October	Everyone	U.S.	Observed in the U.S., Indigenous Peoples' Day serves as a counter-celebration to Columbus Day and honors Native American history and culture.
National Coming Out Day	October 11	Everyone	U.S.	Observed in the U.S., National Coming Out Day supports LGBTQ+ individuals in coming out and features storytelling and visibility campaigns.
Shemini Atzeret/Simchat Torah	22nd day of the Hebrew month of Tishrei. Typically in September or October	Jewish People	Worldwide	Observed by Jews, Simchat Torah is the end of Sukkot and marks the completion and restarting of the Torah reading cycle.
Latina Equal Pay Day	This date symbolizes how far into the year Latina women must work to earn what men earned in the previous year	Everyone	U.S.	Observed in the U.S., Latina Equal Pay Day addresses pay inequity facing Latinas.
Diwali	During the Hindu lunisolar month Kartika. Typically in October or November	Hindus, Jains, and Sikhs	Worldwide	Observed by Hindus, Sikhs, Jains, and others across South Asia, Diwali celebrates the triumph of light over darkness and features lights, sweets, and fireworks.
National American Indian/Alaska Native Heritage Month	November	Everyone	U.S.	Observed in the U.S., National American Indian/Alaska Native Heritage Month recognizes the history and culture of native peoples with events, storytelling, and cultural education.
Veterans Day	November 11	Everyone	U.S.	Observed in the U.S., Veterans Day honors military veterans with parades, speeches, and ceremonies.
Transgender Day of Remembrance	November 20	Everyone	U.S.	Observed globally, Transgender Day of Remembrance honors trans people who have been lost to violence and features vigils and memorial services.

Native American Heritage Day	Fourth Friday of November (Day After Thanksgiving)	Everyone	U.S.	Observed in the U.S., Native American Heritage Day is celebrated on the day after Thanksgiving and recognizes Native American culture and contributions.
World AIDS Day	Decemnber 1	Everyone	Worldwide	Observed globally, World AIDS Day commemorates those lost to HIV/AIDS and raises awareness with vigils, red ribbons, and testing campaigns.
International Day of People with Disabilities	December 3	Everyone	Worldwide	Observed globally, International Day of People with Disabilities promotes inclusion and the rights of individuals with disabilities.
Hanukkah	Begins 25 Kislev and ends 2 Tevet or 3 Tevet on the Jewish calendar. Typically in December or January	Jewish People	Worldwide	Observed by Jews, Hanukkah commemorates the rededication of the Second Temple with nightly menorah lightings, games, and fried foods.
Christmas	December 25	Christians, Non-Christians	Worldwide	Observed by Christians and secular communities worldwide, Christmas celebrates the birth of Jesus and as the season of giving.
Kwanzaa	December 26 - January 1	African-Americans, Africans	Worldwide	Observed by African Americans, Kwanzaa celebrates African heritage and community values.
Guru Gobind Singh Jayanti	December 29	Sikhs	Worldwide, primarily in South Asia	Observed by Sikhs in India and worldwide, Guru Gobind Singh Jayanti commemorates the birth of the tenth Sikh Guru, through prayers, kirtans, and processions.

Scan the QR code to access a digital copy to download and filter to your needs:

Password: DoDEIRight

ACKNOWLEDGEMENTS

I am grateful to the Publish Your Purpose team for its unwavering support and cheerleading, from the very first draft to the final print. I'm particularly grateful to Jenn T. Grace, Brandi Lai, Vikki Brown, Alexander Loutsenko, August Hare, Rebecca Pollock, and Anna Heim.

I could not have done this without the support of Jamey Applegate from Equity At Work™, who masterfully ran the business while I took time to write. Jamey, you are a joy to work with as well as a brilliant DEI consultant, and I am grateful to have you on my team.

I also want to thank our Equity At Work™ clients, who trust us to guide them and walk alongside them in their journeys. You are an inspiration, and it is an honor to work with you.

A special thank you to the many friends and colleagues who cheered me on throughout this process, especially Melissa Flynn Pekar and Sarah Cotton Nelson.

Finally, I want to thank my incredibly supportive husband, Robert, children, Grace and Jack, and bonus kid Harris, who always believe in me and support my endeavors to make the workplace better for everyone. I love you deeply.

ABOUT EQUITY AT WORK™

OUR MISSION

At Equity At Work™, we create innovative, customized solutions for even the most complex DEI challenges. Our mission is to help organizations advance in their DEI journeys so they can have a profound impact on their employees, customers, businesses, and communities. We develop DEI strategies, roadmaps, programs, and first-of-their-kind dashboards, and partner with clients to operationalize DEI throughout their organizations. Our clients outperform their peers in revenue and margin growth, employee engagement, productivity, and retention.

OUR CORE VALUES

- Focused on purpose and impact
- Innovative
- Gritty and resourceful
- Highest integrity with commitment to excellence
- Team and partnership builders

OUR MANIFESTO

Strategic advisor. Business analyst. Equitable employee journey advocate.

A seemingly impossible mixture of idealistic values and real-world pragmatism.

But look closer, and you'll see these things are not incompatible.

Including and equitably advancing employees of all demographics advances business. That is the simple truth Equity At Work™ is built on.

It is the revolutionary insight grasped by companies that are driven not just to succeed but to thrive.

Equity At Work™ is an advisor who helps retain employees across all diversity demographics.

An ally who offers a competitive advantage.

An expert who ensures opportunities are equitable.

A planner who paves the way for the future.

An analyst who uncovers hidden roadblocks.

A messenger delivering priceless information.

A strategist who solves these problems—and in so doing, drives business.

A partner any executive would consider a treasure trove of value.

A company that does all this? That, indeed, is a rare commodity.

A true partner for businesses of every size.

For leaders. For investors. For boards of directors. For all employees.

At Equity for Work™, we are that partner. An advocate for business. And the greater good.

Scan the QR code to access our website, sign up for our newsletter, listen to our Your DEI Minute™ podcast, read The Equity At Work™ blog, and more:

www.equity-at-work.com
hello@equity-at-work.com

The B Corp Movement

Dear Reader,

Thank you for reading this book and joining the Publish Your Purpose community! You are joining a special group of people who aim to make the world a better place.

Certified

(B)

Corporation

What's Publish Your Purpose About?

Our mission is to elevate the voices often excluded from traditional publishing. We intentionally seek out authors and storytellers with diverse backgrounds, life experiences, and unique perspectives to publish books that will make an impact in the world.

Beyond our books, we are focused on tangible, action-based change. As a woman- and LGBTQ+-owned company, we are committed to reducing inequality, lowering levels of poverty, creating a healthier environment, building stronger communities, and creating high-quality jobs with dignity and purpose.

As a Certified B Corporation, we use business as a force for good. We join a community of mission-driven companies building a more equitable, inclusive, and sustainable global economy. B Corporations must meet high standards of transparency, social and environmental performance, and accountability as determined by the nonprofit B Lab. The certification process is rigorous and ongoing (with a recertification requirement every three years).

How Do We Do This?

We intentionally partner with socially and economically disadvantaged businesses that meet our sustainability goals. We embrace and encourage our authors and employee's differences in race, age, color, disability, ethnicity, family or marital status, gender identity or expression, language, national origin, physical and mental ability, political affiliation, religion, sexual orientation, socio-economic status, veteran status, and other characteristics that make them unique.

Community is at the heart of everything we do—from our writing and publishing programs to contributing to social enterprise nonprofits like reSET (www.resetco. org) and our work in founding B Local Connecticut.

We are endlessly grateful to our authors, readers, and local community for being the driving force behind the equitable and sustainable world we are building together.

To connect with us online or publish with us, visit us at www.publishyourpurpose.com.

Elevating Your Voice,

Jenn T Grace

Jenn T. Grace
Founder, Publish Your Purpose

www.ingramcontent.com/pod-product-compliance
Lightning Source LLC
Chambersburg PA
CBHW041732200326

41518CB00019B/2574